Contents

Got Carrots? ® ii

Epigraph xi

Dedication xiii

Preface xv

Introduction xvii

    Positive Training Environments.............................. xviii

    Goals and Objectives xix

    Training or Retraining xx

    There Are No Perfect Horses xx

    Using **Applied** Behavior Analysis........................... xxi

    Risk Management xxi

    Critical Thinking xxii

    Case Study Examples xxiii

PART I

Introduction to Positive Horses 1

    The Method Using Positive Reinforcement................ 2

    Method of Positive Reinforcement........................... 3

Teaching Important Cues: Come, Stand, Walk-On, Halt........ 9

Perfect Practice Makes Perfect 17

Perfect Timing 21

Correct Longe Work 25

Successfully Using Rider Aids 29

    Behavior Modification for Serious Riders Aids 30

Explanation of Rider Aids 32
Rider Rein Aids -The Secret of Using a Half-Halt..........................34
    Importance of Negative Reinforcer..36
Equestrian Literature..39

PART II

Benefits of Working With Horses and Carts...................................49
    Potential for More Interest in Driving 50
    Fox lessons: Beginning Work With a Carriage/
    Training Cart..51
    Summary 84
Firestar and the 'Yahoo'..85
Jewel: A Case Study-Reversing 91
Story of Great Dane Allie Teaching a Safety Cue 103

Books by Patti Dammier PhD..109
Afterword...111
About the Author 113
Glossary 115
References 119
Index..123

List of Tables

Table 1 Relationship Between Behavior and Rewards.........................4

Table 2 Cue, Behavior, Reward Primary and Secondary...................5

Table 3 Aversive /Punishment...7

Table 4 Contingencies —Comparison Results..............................7

Table 5 Cue Behavior Consequence...11

Table 6 Horse Stands on Cue 13

Table 7 Negative Reinforcer Rider Aids Using the Reins.................19

Table 8 Negative Reinforcer 33

Table 9 Half-Halt..36

Table 10 Negative Reinforcement – Use of Reins............................37

Table 11 Teaching Horse to Come on Cue 92

Table 12 Teaching the Horse the Cue 'Walk on'.............................95

Notes: Cover Picture Horse

The horse pictured on the book's cover and also used for many of the photographs/cartoons for the Got Carrots?® series of books, including the cover for the series *Got Carrots?* ®*Rescued Horse*, is the lovely Hungarian Mare named Firebird. She is the offspring of the German mare Fanfare von Harnish and the Hungarian stallion Wistar.

> The story of these [Hungarian] horses begins back in Hungary in an era when horses were considered part of a country's national treasure. In times of war, the breeding stock from the national Stud Farms was displaced in order to save them from destruction or capture. One link in the long saga was the rescuing of Hungarian horses, along with the Lipizzaners, by General Patton from what was to be the Russian zone. Once these horses arrived in Occupied Germany, a group of them was selected by Colonel Hamilton, Chief of the US Remount Service, to be sent to the United States to improve the breeding stock in the US Army Remount Breeding program. In 1949, the Remount Program was disbanded and again, if it wasn't for some quick action on the part of Countess Margit Sigray-Bessenyey, the Cooksleys, and Jim Edwards, these horses might have been lost.
>
> (The American Hungarian Horse Association)

Epigraph

Horses should be trained in such a way that they not only love their riders but look forward to the time they are with them.

—Xenophon 400 BC

Dedication

To my husband, Ernie, a very special source of encouragement, my mother, Marion, who taught me to love and respect animals, and Xerxio, a gifted and wonderful horse, one of many who inspired me in my pursuit.

Preface

The following paragraph summarizes my continued interest to promote a "positive method for training horses", as used in previous book titles to describe an educationally behavioral approach to learning.

> My pursuit of creating positive educational environments that support learning has lead to a lifelong study both experiential and academic. People or animals engage in activities that are pleasant and are encouraged to repeat those activities because they're pleasant. There is nothing mysterious about how learning takes place and the methods that will reinforce those preferred behaviors. Just because horse training claims to be natural doesn't mean it's an effective tool for creating a learning environment for horses. Horses accept our intervention because they learn through a series of positive experiences that no harm comes to them and we are consistent in our positive behavior. Research demonstrates that horses respond favorably to humans because we create a positive relationship.
>
> It's time to move away from the faddish and quick fix methods and invest a little time to learn the **basic principles of behavior modification** that teaches anyone to create a **positive** learning environment and a method of obtaining desirable behavior from horses.
>
> (Dammier,2019,xv)

At the beginning of logical training the rider becomes acquainted with his horse and learns to understand him.
                                        —Alois Podhajsky

Introduction

Horse training isn't a mystical procedure. In fact, there isn't mystery in the methods necessary to teach any skill. To learn any skill there is a logical sequence that if adhered to, allows a behavior to be taught and learned. Creating a **Positive Horse** consists of using positive methods, which in turn creates a positive attitude. This book explains those positive methods necessary to create horses that perform on taught/learned cues, both on the ground and in the saddle that are systematically rewarded, but also that have an extremely positive attitude to their trainer/companion. The system uses the method, 'Behavior Modification'.

Positive Horses is about:

- Explanation of basic educational methods using systematic sequences that support training horses.
- Creating the goals and objectives for each individual horse rather than a "one size fits all" approach.
- Training using positive reinforcement— how food rewards creates useable cues, instead of the trainer performing meaningless behavior that the horse doesn't understand.
- Initially using primary rewards to teach cues strengthens learning.
- Horses learning basic cues: come, stand, walk on, and halt, which provides safety on the ground and assists in the next work in the saddle.

- Basic training is easily applied to a variety of equestrian disciplines.
- Addressing training method failure, because the trainer doesn't assess the correct the behavior to reward and doesn't understand the methods.
- Horse case studies exemplifying the use of behavioral methods.

This book is designed for the person who wants to learn an educated approach based on scientific theory. The outlined training contained in this book uses the research and resources of the disciplines of learning and education rather than the latest hype and mysticism. Even though we feel an emotional connection with our equine partner, this doesn't preclude relying on systematic educational procedures, especially when we use positive methods.

The majority of horse training books outline a routine procedure that the trainer has found to be successful. In many cases, these may serve as a resource for ideas. However, what is missing from these training methods are the basic educational principles that allow the trainer to create their own training procedure tailored for their own horse, and the explanation why the method works. Horses have individual differences depending on past experience, so they don't come to a training session with a clean blank slate; this includes heredity, and random learning.

When a horse doesn't respond with what most folks expect, the use of behavior analysis allows the trainer to view the horse behavior in terms as shapeable, changeable, and doable responses. Even with well-trained horses unfortunate occurrences may happened, as you will read in several case studies about horses with previous experiences.

Positive Training Environments

- All positive systematic learning environments create a productive, positive atmosphere and hopefully knowledgeable decisions about desired behavior

- The environment is created for successful learning starting with keeping distractions reduced at the beginning
- Decide on a single observable behavior to be learned
- Describe the single behavior in observable terms
- Practice the single behavior until learned
- Use the practice of behavior modification with taught cues and rewards

The first considerations should be: What do I want my horse to learn?... What is the horse able to learn?

Often the trainer launches the first ideas from a training method without considering what do I want my horse to learn and more important what can the horse learn. What works in the latest horse training fad or hyped horse magazine article may not work for your horse or you're having problems not outlined in the 'canned lesson'. Not every horse reacts the same way to the same lesson. For example, a trainer may be able to bridle, saddle, and ride a horse in one session. Should this be the template lesson for every horse owner? I hope not, because considering a risk management model this is a dangerous practice as it is for many sports/hobbies.

Goals and Objectives

The difference between a goal and objective should be clearly understood, because it helps the trainer decide on the specifics of the skills for the training session. "Riders and trainers often set large broad goals, but fail to break these goals down into the smallest objective or successful act the horse can perform. Not only is it important to have a clear picture of the broad goal of your training but also the small steps that lead to that goal" (Dammier, 2001, p. 16).

Each small step then is described in the specific skill/behavior that is taught. If the **goal** is to have a horse that pulls a small cart then the specific behaviors are described and taught. (See: Fox lessons: Beginning

Work with a Carriage/Training Cart) To be an effective trainer there has to be a clear idea of what is being taught—this is true for all teaching whether it's flying, reading, research …or other exacting activities. Frequently the trainer must stop and reevaluate the training lesson with a new task or training objective. This book will explain how to create those individualized training skills for your horse.

Training or Retraining

Many horse owners are working with a previously owned horse or have begun training a young horse that had an improper response, which became a poor habit. With the rare exception of the vicious horse, those who have been severely punished and abused, there are many poorly trained horses that may have a new life with a systematic *"Horse Makeover"*. Whether the trainer is working from the beginning or retraining there are important decisions to be made as each horse progresses with their own unique talents and problems.

There Are No Perfect Horses

Despite what you may have read, not only are there 'no perfect horses' and also there are 'no perfect trainers'. Luckily, there are methods that allow us to reevaluate how the training procedures may be changed. Keeping this in mind, any horse training procedure should ask following questions:

Questions to Consider

- What is the overall goal for this horse?
- What are the specific single tasks or behaviors that the horse can/will learn?
- Are these tasks or behaviors suitable and at the level for this horse?

- How are these single tasks or behaviors linked together to create more complicated performance?
- What are the systematic methods for increasing or decreasing desired or undesirable behavior?
- Is the single behavior being taught perfectly practiced on a regular schedule before moving to more difficult tasks?
- What are the consequences of my actions or risk for this training session?
- What might be the risk to horse or rider if safe procedures aren't followed?

Using Applied Behavior Analysis

Rather than using rote methods for teaching horse behavior there are many research and written materials that explain how animals learn. The foundation of learning theory and how animals learn is explained by applied behavior analysis and the methods of behavior modification and operant conditioning.

A simple explanation of these principles is that behavior followed by an event, such as a reinforcer (commonly called rewards), will increase the occurrence of that behavior. When this behavior is connected to a cue (a reminder), the cue becomes a training tool. The solution of many horse training problems is answered by teaching new cues using systematic behavioral methods. As in all my books, including *Behavior Modification for Horses* and *Horse Makeovers*, there are several chapters with case studies describing these principles and how they may be used for changing horse behavior.

Risk Management

Working with horses has the possibility of inherent danger. While their nature is normally placid, horses are large animals with keen survival reflexes. The fight and flight response is at the heart of the survival of a horse and the goal of training is to replace these automatic responses with new behaviors that are learned using behavior modification. It's remarkable to observe that horses even when disrupted from their routine will respond to learned cues. This is why it's important to create these cues without using gadgets that you will not have with you when a horse suddenly is running free.

Most dangerous occupations always put a risk management plan in place. Aside from the occasional comments about potential danger, there is little written about approaching working with horses from a risk management advantage. All dangerous professions approach training environments by reducing potential risk to life and limb by choosing safe environments and procedures. Horse training should be no exception. There are many ways to work with the horse in a safe manner before rushing into a dangerous riding situation.

Unfortunately, the cultural aspects of the old west, even with the new marketing hype to make it appear kinder and gentler, are still present where young horses are quickly ridden without adequate preparation. Research documents demonstrate that repetition is required to consider a skill learned. This book will include the many ways the trainer may safely prepare for work in the saddle especially with inexperienced and retraining mounts.

Critical Thinking

There has been a recent trend toward accepting ideas that sound glamorous and make us feel good. They are appealing in that they appear to make everything right with little effort or work. The learning sequence should be approached with evaluation and assessment. Much horse training relies on rote learning, which depends on repetition. While this repetition provides consistency, there are instances where the learning process doesn't run a straight course compatible with rote learning. If a rote method is followed without considering unique variances, eventually there will be a point of learning impasse. Unfortunately, this is the point where many trainers resort to force or aversive control. As explained in chapter two, aversive/punishing control may result in serious unintended consequences.

Successful teachers/trainers should be aware of the constant change in the learning environment and the relationship of the trainer to this environment. Since the trainer may not have had the experience with an individual problem posed in a horse-training situation, they may use the tool of applied behavior analysis to assess the performance. Applied behavior analysis means: "The behaviors operate on the environment and have consequences that affect the likelihood that they are performed in the future" (Kazdin,1994, p. 25). The significance is that the observed horse behavior is analyzed using critical thinking and the trainer develops a unique way of solving the problem instead of persisting with an unsuccessful rote method.

Horses do well with rote learning, because they are successful with few changes. However, it can be observed that some of the difficulties with horses happen when we change the routine or the environment. This is why it's necessary to have several strong learned cues as the example of the safety/stand cue and the means to understand the impact of the environment including the trainer's influence on horse performance (see story about Fox and the student, and how a learned cue saved the day).

Critical thinking is the ability to analyze a situation and make decisions based on that information. Rather than approaching training merely as a rote method it's beneficial for the trainer to continually evaluate the progress of the horse. As humans have a variety of talents and traits, horses likewise demonstrate those variations. In view of this variety of talents it's important to critically think about each horse's individual training program.

Case Study Examples

The case studies of several horses are included to give the reader examples of educational training plans using applied behavior analysis. A specific behavioral plan is created and used in the instruction of the horse. Each horse case study comes from horses that have had difficulties encountered by their owner with a description of the problem; the plan of action and the results. The range are: horses needing retraining of improper aids, young horses that spontaneously resist training, and horses exposed to a random negative occurrence. There are safe methods to retrain horses using correct positive methods.

Options for Reading this Book

This book is written in two parts giving the reader the option for the reading order. The reader may choose to read the educational groundwork first and then read the case studies. If the reader desires, they may read the case studies first, getting an idea of the implementation and return to the first section to study the educational basis. I would strongly urge the reader, no matter which order they choose, to review carefully Part I to have a solid understanding of the basic principles of learning theory.

Part I

Introduction to Positive Horses

Positive trained horses perform extremely well because they have learned systematic skills/cues confidently with their trainer, because of the positive cue and consequences connected with the training.

Positive consequences consist of:

1. Perfectly timing food rewards beginning with easy to learn desired behavior
2. Connected with a cue
3. Progressing to more complicated series of behaviors that don't need food rewards.

Each time the horse sees their trainer they know it will be a pleasant experience, besides the taught cue the trainer is always there and becomes an additional positive cue. For example read about Jewel, a beautiful Hungarian horse that learned to come and stand on cue. This first session was accomplished right after she was scared. This made working with the slightly fearful Jewel safer to handle on the ground; to start beginning training and will make it easier to safely train her for saddle work. Her owner was rightly worried about being on the ground nearby.

*Each time the horse sees their trainer they know
it will be a pleasant experience.*

There are many ways to accomplish creating confidence with your horse. Often horse confidence randomly occurs without any forethought by the trainer. The trainer being a calm easygoing quiet horse person will likewise produce a confident horse. Nevertheless, there are systematic methods to produce the lesson for creating horse confidence, which generate the ability to teach the horse new skills quickly that are permanently remembered. Basic skill training is the sequential system of building skills one upon the other and systematically reinforcing them. This book will explain these methods. This book is separated into two sections: methods and case studies.

The Method Using Positive Reinforcement

Despite what you've been told horses don't bite because of hand feeding them any more than dogs will bite because they've been fed treats. Horses <u>will</u> bite if they are allowed to grab rewards as dogs <u>will</u> bite due to inadequate training. For some reason folks will teach dogs to take a treat gently, but there is little understanding that horses are smart enough to learn the same rules.

There are examples horse training methods described as nonviolent, but these methods describe chasing a horse as if a predator, and throwing ropes and shaking plastic bags to make them move forward. An important cue for horses of any discipline is to move forward on an **established cue**. Why would a trainer perform actions to make this important action anything but a consistent quietly learned cue?

Method of Positive Reinforcement

Horse trainers who try the methods of operant conditioning, which use rewards paired with desired behavior, find a quick effective way of teaching horses cues.

The research from the 1940s, called operant conditioning, outlines a series of operations to increase or decrease behavior. The horse is taught a single cue. A single cue is connected to a simple behavior and immediately rewarded. The cue is taught so the trainer isn't running around trying to figure out how to make the horse perform simple cues such as come, stand, walk-on, and halt.

There is a difference between being observant of horse behavior and using that knowledge rather than basing horse training on trying merely to guess the significance of the observation. The practical method is to teach a specific cue for the desired horse behavior. Instead of waiting or chasing your child, you want to call their name and have them come; it's a safety factor as it is with your horse. If the trainer merely tries to figure out what the horse is thinking, and wanders around trying to do something, the lesson will at best be vague. The horse may decide he feels confident or take a defiant stance of protection out of fear. This is why chasing horses and throwing ropes at them is to risk making the horse fear you as a predator. A confident building procedure for teaching the horse a cue provides a positive systematic method. Why would you come to the person who throws things at you?

Horses demonstrate unique characteristics (species specific behavior) for training that is different from other animals. Unlike other animals that are primarily trained on the ground, horses will eventually be ridden or trained for carriage work. Even though the principles of behavior modification work for animals and humans, each category needs attention to those specific differences to be effective. To assume that dog training principles may be exactly applied to horses is in error. While the main methods may be accurate, the specific behavior of each is different; mainly horses are ridden.

The following chapter is a condensed outline of the important parts of behavior modification needed to train horses:

Table 1 Relationship Between Behavior and Rewards
(Dammier, 2001, p.29)

Desired Behavior	Reward/ Positive Reinforcers
	Given immediately upon the behavior every time until behavior is learned

1. **Positive reinforcers** – commonly called **rewards**

   a. Primary – rewards that don't need to be taught –food
   b. Secondary – 'stand-in' rewards that are connected with food and previously taught to continue reinforce training
      1. The gadget techniques, while fine with dogs, are a waste of time, because serious riders want to use their cues/ 'stand-in' rewards in the saddle.
      2. It is a waste of time dragging a gadget around –when you have a serious situation – you don't want to worry about a gadget. The horse should be trained with cues/ 'stand-in' rewards that you always have with you. Watch some of the great trick horse movies — they weren't lugging around a gadget, but rather they used sight and sound cues.
      3. Think about the critical situation with Allie (Part II) sound and taught cues were all present—didn't have any gadgets with me.
      4. If the traditional sounds used with horses are paired with primary/food reinforcers, they become the stand-in reward

that doesn't need a gadget. While training on the ground these sounds may be taught and then used while riding.

5. See the case studies for specific applications.

The following outlines the systematic method for beginning to teach a single cue using a primary reward:

1. A cue is decided
2. The horse demonstrates the behavior
3. The consequence is a real tangible reward— one the horse doesn't have to be taught–– the reward secures the behavior as the horse makes a clear connection to the cue and behavior
4. This is also explained in textbooks as the ABC procedure: Antecedent, Behavior, and Consequence

Table 2 Cue, Behavior, Reward Primary and Secondary

Cue (antecedent)	Behavior	Consequence – Tangible Reward

The following outline is a description of how the **secondary** or **stand-in** reward can be taught. After the horse performs upon giving the decided cue, the real reward is given along with a stand-in.

Cue	Behavior	Consequence –
		Tangible Reward includes the stand-in paired with the tangible food reward

2. **Negative reinforcers** (**Rider aids**) – a slightly unpleasant action– when removed **increases** the behavior that follows the release of the negative action or cue. Most rider aids are negative reinforcers.

    a. It's called a negative reinforcer, because when the action is **stopped** it **rewards** or reinforces the behavior that follows so that the desired behavior is more likely to occur again.

    b. This is very important because most of the cues given from the saddle fit this description–an action of the reins on the bridle.

    c. This is one the most misunderstood concepts in behavior modification– most equestrians will **not** spend most of their time on the ground, much in the way dogs are trained.

    d. The rider aid of using a **Half- halt** is an example of a negative reinforcer used to various degrees in equitation disciplines. The half-halt is also the basis for the exercises used in the equestrian disciplines to communicate through the use of reins.

3. **Aversive control**—commonly called punishment – is a consequence or action that stops or ceases the behavior. "Punishment can be an effective tool to stop negative behavior so that a trainer may proceed to a reward situation" (Dammier, 2019 p. 38).

    a. Aversive control should be extremely cautiously used— there are other methods that are potentially more effective—this is for horses (and people) for similar reasons.

    b. Punishment potentially has unsatisfactory consequences if not absolutely correctly implemented.

    c. Punishment should be absolutely connected with the action.

    d. Research demonstrates it is applied within seconds rule.

    e. If the action of punishment fails to **stop or decrease** the inappropriate behavior ––the behavior may be actually strengthened as the horse learns they may escape performing.

    f. As with food rewards that become associated with the person, punishment also becomes associated with the person.

    g. If punishment is effective it works the first time and doesn't need to be repeated.

Table 3 Aversive /Punishment

Undesired **Behavior**	**Aversive / Punishment** consequence –given immediately after the behavior –stop behavior –removes it from the repertoire

The practical usage of an aversive stimulus used for the safety of enclosing horses is the electrically charged fence wire. The horse, immediately upon touching the wire near the fence, is given a small unpleasant shock and stays away from the fence. This description is one example of how an aversive stimulus or control can provide a positive benefit and keep our partners out of harm's way. The other aspect is the cue, which is the fence, is not associated with the trainer (Dammier, 2019, p. 39).

Remember swatting horses is subject to the split-second timing with the behavior——if you're going to swat for inappropriate behavior it must be **exactly** connected to the behavior, otherwise you have a ducking, shying horse every time you move your hand. You just became an aversive cue.

Table 4 Contingencies —Comparison Results

# 1 Positive Reinforcer/ Reward	#2 Negative Reinforcer	#3 Aversive control/ punishment
Strengthen or increases the behavior	*****Strengthens** or increases the behavior that reduces or stops the negative reinforcer	*****Stops** or **weakens** the learned behavior

*****Notice** the comparison that the aversive contingencies have a different outcome —there is often confusion about the negative reinforcer—rider aids and the contingency of aversive or punishment. Often trainers are confused about the implementation and outcome. If a punishment/aversive control is used and doesn't stop the behavior, it has failed in the outcome. Trainers often think this failure means they only have to do the action harder. Rewarding incompatible behavior is much more successful —remember a horse can't be simultaneously nipping and standing at attention.

Key Points

- This section outlines the main methods for changing horse behavior using behavior modification for horses.
- Actions performed by the trainer have consequences and should be seriously thought out in advance.
- Random happenings also have consequences.
- Constant aversive control invites retaliation.
- Equestrians, while handling horse on the ground, also handle the horse while riding and should think about logical sequences that work for both.
- Teaching basic cues such as come and stand provide a safe environment on the ground and transform into riding work — we teach all the horses to stand on cue so mounting becomes as simple of giving the cue.
- Understanding the principles of behavior modification allows trainers completely to create a unique training situation and **positive horses.**

Teaching Important Cues: Come, Stand, Walk-On, Halt

There are four important cues to work with horses safely on the ground: Come, Stand, Walk-on, and Halt. It is simply ridiculous to stand around and wait for a horse to decide to come to you, when this behavior may be taught and become a cue for the horse to come anywhere— not only when trapped in a pen.

Most horses when trapped in a small area, if they haven't had negative experiences with humans, will come to the person quietly standing in the pen. While this procedure can produce a trusting horse; however, teaching the horse a cue to come gives permanence to a taught signal that may be used in different places and eventually free in a pasture. Horses can be taught to run to the trainer from the far side of a pasture, **not** by shaking a grain bucket but on a taught hand/sound cue. How will the horse be caught if there is no grain bucket available?

The behavioral methods described are used successfully with many animals. The industries such as animal movie stars use the techniques to teach cues to create permanent commands. Many movie star horses are taught cues to perform. Unfortunately this systematic method doesn't seem to be used with sport horses. The following method was used with the training of the mare Jewel, described in the case study section part II, so the mare could be safely handled. These four steps are also used in teaching Fox to drive a training cart. His ability to stand on cue made it fairly easy to introduce him to the cart and also later to have him stand quietly when being harnessed.

Step 1

The first step is to teach the horse to come to the trainer on cue.

1. The trainer stands in front of the horse close enough for the horse to take a step in that direction.
2. The trainer decides on a sound and or visual cue – any suitable cue easily recognized.
3. If a sound cue is used, it should be said consistently.
4. As soon as the horse moves toward to the trainer, a food treat is presented immediately when performing the behavior.
5. The trainer decides on food that they know the horse will like. With very young horses a handful of grain can be used. Later we progressed to carrots, because we found that they all liked carrots. Folks use other items.
6. It's important to start with a reward that **doesn't** need to be taught. Food rewards are called a **primary reinforcer**, because they don't need to be taught. Good girl/boy or pats have **no** meaning to the horse. An untrained horse might be frightened of a pat. Later this pat can be parried with the food reward and the horse makes a pleasant connection with the pat or soft words; it becomes the stand-in reward.
7. Later after the trainer observes that the horse understands the cue to "come" the schedule of rewarding with food will change frequency, but until the horse performs on each request the food reward/primary reward is given on each performance.
8. Later the schedule will change to what is called a **secondary reinforcer** or "stand-in" reward, which may be taught after the cue is understood. This is when the good girl/boy and pat becomes stand-in for the food reward.
9. The food reward is only used to start the learning process.
10. Just as I know where my secret stash of my favorite cookies is hidden, horses will begin to seek where the reward is hidden.
11. Food rewards are **very** powerful which is why animals quickly learn new behaviors—instead of trainers walking around waiting for the horse to figure out what we want.

Table 5 Cue Behavior Consequence

Cue/ Stimulus	Behavior	Consequence.
Signal or cue decided to be used	Horse takes a few steps	Horse is immediately rewarded upon the behavior of stepping forward to the handler

Step 2
The next step is to teach the horse to stand on cue.

This cue to stand on cue is also described in my book *Horse Makeovers* (Dammier, 2014, p.17) as a safety cue. Anytime the horse is not focused on the trainer, the cue can be use to get the horse to stand. This is valuable because if a horse is standing quietly they can't simultaneously engage in undesirable actions (incompatible behavior). Many times trainers resort to punishment that isn't needed to obtain horse compliance. Horses while not tied in their stalls, make tasks easier by standing on cue. This saves time in an already tight schedule. This cue transfers when the horse is mounted, attached to carts, and they need to stand quietly. There is no force involved, and the horses are taught the stand cue at liberty: first in their stall and later in other spaces.

1. In a quiet place the horse is given the command to "stand", including a sight cue such as a raised arm. Horses easily learn both sight and sound cues.
2. As soon as the horse to stand —reward with the favorite food.
3. Using the "come" command ask the horse to take steps and reward—ensure the horse understands the cue to come. This is normally taught in about 5 minutes.
4. Give the command to "stand" and reward.
5. The horse normally becomes very interested in the lessons because of the food and begins to look for where it is hidden. The trainer should now start to handle the horse with the support of a whip. This whip will never strike the horse but be used as a pointer. If the horse looks to take the reward the trainer will quietly hold the whip in-between to direct the horse away. As soon as the horse responds correctly—the reward is given. The whip is now introduced in a non-threateningly manner and can be used confidently later in other exercises. The horses on the farm are so accustomed to the benign use of whips they're totally confident.
6. Horses that haven't had ropes thrown at them, trainers yelling, or smacking with the hands will learn the correct use of the whip, which will be taught as a directional aid.
7. The correct quiet use of the whip becomes synonymous with the positively taught cues.
8. It is extremely important that the reward is **only** given for the correct response.
9. Using a food reward is extremely powerful.
10. The whole process becomes positive when approached by systematic rewarding the correct behavior.
11. Words need to be consistently and clearly pronounced—and unique.

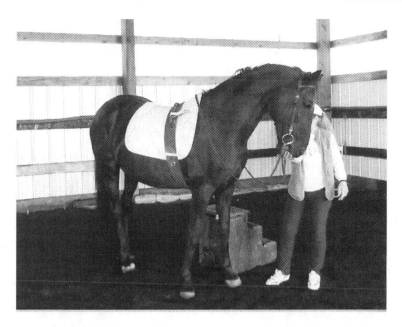

Table 6 Horse Stands on Cue

Cue/Stimulus	Behavior	Consequence-Reward
The cue for horse to stand—a sound and hand signal.	Horse standing quietly— this is progressively extended—eventually the trainer can walk around the horse and the horse will continue to stand.	A piece of carrot or other food is given as soon as the horse stands quietly not looking at the trainer.

Step 3 and step 4

These two cues can be taught together and provide the skills that are necessary to begin safely walking your horse and eventually teaching them to work on the longe correctly with the use of correct rider aids. The aids taught on the ground will consistently be used with other horse training and as work progresses in the saddle.

Step 3

1. Standing by the horse's shoulder —give the command using a sound cue and motioning with the whip. Since the horse has been familiarized to the whip being used as an aid in previous lessons and the horse doesn't fear the trainer —the correct aid will show the horse the direction to move forward. This why it's important that no one has thrown ropes, yelled, or chased the horse as a predator.
2. Part of the lesson is to learn the correct aids: voice, whip, lead line.
3. The exercise is performed along a wall– using the fence or wall as a guide.

4. The horse is being taught to "walk on" on a sound command–
   this will be used for all training when mounted, driving, or
   leading that requires that the horse walk forward on a cue.
5. Leading a horse is not accomplished by dragging them around
   but by teaching the horse to move forward on a command with
   the trainer in a safe place at the shoulder.
6. The horse is rewarded (primary and stand-in) on completion
   of action.
7. Common sounds used to encourage a horse to move forward
   are taught on the ground and later used for other skills in the
   saddle.

Step 4

1. After the horse takes several steps forward —on a sound cue and
   a slight restraining vibration motion on the halter—ask/signal
   using a cue— the horse to stop and reward immediately. The
   horse will also catch the less obvious cue of the trainer moving
   forward and stopping.
2. This becomes a two-step process of walk a few steps and halt––
   immediately reward the horse upon stopping. If the horse looks
   for the reward the hand/whip simply quietly blocks the motion
   and waits until the horse looks forward.

Key Points

- Taught cues both sight and sounds are learned skills for both
  the horse and the trainer.
- The horse gets instant feedback about correct responses
  reinforced with rewards by using a series of reinforcers.
- While working with established cues, the horse has confidence
  in a positive environment.
- The trainer becomes skilled in observing horse behaviors and
  tailoring the lesson to fit the horse.

- In beginning of teaching new skills correct mistakes are rewarded—if the horse halts the behavior is accepted, because it means the horse is attempting to perform what the trainer wants. The horse is quietly asked again. Often the horse will turn toward the trainer; the trainer merely quietly returns to the starting point and asks again.
- Quiet corrections support the horse's confidence and positive environment.
- At the beginning of teaching new skills, the cues and rewards should be timed exactly when applied.
- Recognize that trainer becomes a part of the cue and the reward— my horses know I dispense food just like your kids/friends know where you keep the candy bars.
- The horse has learned to work safely along side the trainer "in hand" with confidence in the trainer.
- The trainer can refocus the horse on a learned cue rather than hoping or in suspense that things will turn out okay.
- All this work carries over to the other disciplines such as riding and driving carriages.
- New skills are practiced in small quiet places where the environment helps shape behavior.
- Read specifics of these four cues in the Jewel case study.

Perfect Practice
Makes Perfect

Having competed in national equestrian events in Europe, it became clear that serious riders have an understanding of how complex horse behaviors may be taught. This includes all the equitation disciplines that require what is explained as **rider aids** in most literature. When the rider picks up the reins, the expert rider whether or not they can explain their methods, should understand the behavior dynamics of the reins in connection to horse performance. Often the effective methods required are much different than explained by the commonly promoted training methods, because the trainers don't understand the behavioral relationship of their aids and horse performance.

Actually their horses teach the trainers. If the horse performs the desired behavior the trainers thinks this works—good trainer. However, if the horse doesn't perform what always seemed to work for the trainer— bad horse. The trainer at this point attempts to repeat what didn't work because the trainer thinks it must be done more forcefully. This is where the concept of '**perfect practice**' explains how learning takes place.

There are several points that explain how horses or anyone learns complex behavior:

1. The new behavior should be simple and clearly understood.
2. There is an important part about practice — the new skill should be practiced correctly.
3. The length of the practice isn't as significant as the correct quality—**perfect practice makes perfect.**
4. Ending a lesson on the best performance is important.

While there are various aspects to riding, an explanation of rider aids should be addressed. The simple fact is: All riders include some mild reminders to the horse that is a command, cue, or called '**rider aids**'. No matter what your riding discipline, there is an important overlooked aspect of these riders' aids. Before beginning describing the scientific facts that operate ridden horse behavior—**rider aids**, the following is important:

1. Teaching any complicated series of behaviors means the animal understands what is asked and has the skills to perform those tasks. This is the teaching technique that is effectively used to teach anyone difficult tasks including, flying airplanes, teaching reading to young children, performing dance steps……etc.
2. A simple description of the rider rein aid is: The rider gives the cue and as soon as the horse responds the mildly asking aid is stopped on the correct horse response.

Do Rider Aids Encourage Perfect Performance?

What is the significance of the behavioral concept of the **negative reinforcer** to the **rider aids** of using reins?

Even though the words seem to be a contradiction in meaning, a simple way to describe a **negative reinforcer** could be translated into a mildly unpleasant cue that when stopped encourages, increases, or rewards the behavior that follows the mildly unpleasant cue. The mildly unpleasant cue, if it is to be effective, should produce **immediate results** and **increase** the following desired behavior. This is important to understand, because if the mildly unpleasant cue doesn't produce the desired behavior, the cue or desired behavior is not correct. Horses tend to remember both positive and negative learned behavior, which is why training should focus on correct responses.

The following table gives the scientific explanation for a **Negative Reinforcer** is: Outlined in *Behavior Modification for Horses*. (Dammier 2001, p. 126).

Table 7 Negative Reinforcer Rider Aids Using the Reins

Cue
Reins in contact with the horse's mouth

▪ Behavior
The horse yields and lightens contact

▪ Consequence
Reins release contact to the horse's mouth– the horses learns the correct response to the rider command

Key Points

- In order to have perfect practice, much of successful horse training incorporates a sequential range of skills that begins with the easiest mastered and progresses to the more difficult as the horse is able to perform those behaviors. This encourages the horse to practice what is desired.
- The horse is taught understandable cues that are implemented with the least force to encourage a positive learning environment. This reduces an environment of escalating force and focuses on correctly learned skills.
- The cues are taught by quiet repetition and not by scaring or frightening the horse into performing. For example horses are taught the cue to move forward, which can begin on the ground and continue with correct longe work including the correct use of the whip—not by throwing things, using plastic bags, and other frightening objects.
- The use of the whip becomes a non-threatening tool and a rider aid.
- Since some of the rider aids use mildly unpleasant cues, these cues are given with the **least** amount of force.
- Mildly unpleasant cues, which may be described as a negative reinforcers are immediately stopped on correct horse performance, increasing the maximum horse practice.
- Rider Aids are critical in creating perfect practice.

Perfect Timing

One of the most important and often overlooked aspects of using reward or punishing consequences of rider aids is the **perfect timing** that supports perfect practice. The expert riders pictured in the photo exhibiting the *Alter- Real* horses from the Equestrian School of Alter do Chao, Portugal, exemplifies the art of infinitesimal rider aids. I was fortunate to study at this exceptional training establishment where riders are taught the perfect timing of rider aids.

Whether or not the rider has used primary rewards to strengthen cues, those taught cues will become important for every step of training. When the horse is asked for a basic halt, the quality of that training will be self-evident. As in the above picture, both horses are relaxed with no tension.

The account of "wait until your father comes home" is an example of a practice used with children. This delayed timing punishment factor when used with children has a slight consequence as an imminent threat, but when used with animals is nonsense, because they can't remember two seconds after the behavior.

Important rule: Any consequence should immediately follow behavior to be effective––this includes what are commonly called rewards, punishments, and the release of an unpleasant cue —negative reinforcers. Perfect timing is at the core of training effectiveness, positive horses, and the art of highly trained equestrians.

During my riding experiences in Spain some of equestrian tools/riders aids such as whips and spurs came into question. One of the examples occurred when a rider brought a horse up to a jump and the horse refused. The rider turned the horse around and brought the horse directly in front of the jump and proceeded to graze the horse with the spurs while wildly and angrily whipping the horse on the head. This was important a turning point, because up until this moment, nothing had ever happened to the riders for this type of unsportsmanlike behavior. This instance was a very important because it changed how competitors behaved during events.

Over the announcement system came the following: Rider eliminated for improper use of the spurs and whip. Now if a rider injuriously used the rider aids they would forfeit the competition. This included all the areas on the grounds including the warm-up areas. This was a step forward to enforce the rules of good horsemanship and the **aversive** consequences would now be leveled on the rider not the horse. An example of the perfectly timed consequence: rider elimination!

Besides the important aspect of viciousness to the horse, there is an also important principle of the use of rewards and punishment. In chapter three the specifics of reward and punishment are outlined. In addition, the importance aspects of timing in order to correctly use reinforcement/aversive control methods there are extremely essential. They can't be implemented haphazardly. Many folks believe if you hand feed horses they will bite. Yes, they will bite if you give them food when they grab it from you. This is the important aspect of timing. Reward must be timed with behavior.

It was noted while visiting our veterinarian office for an introductory visit for a large easily excitable young dog that she was greeted with treats. The interesting disparity was noted that even though we know that dogs may bite, their human owners do not have a problem lavishing treats on their canine pet. However, the owners of horses often deny their pets the treats, because they think that they'll learn to bite

Actually both dogs and horses share some similar behaviors in that food is a reward that **doesn't** need to be taught. Both horses and dogs immediately understand the benefit of food when presented. This means that when food is presented during a behavior it will be repeated because the animal seeks the repetition of receiving food. A dog will learn to sit in a five-minute lesson if the treat is clearly presented and timed with the behavior. The same sequence is true to teach a horse to stand on a given cue.

This is an example of how timing becomes an important factor for learning. If the command to sit/stand and the reward isn't perfectly timed the learned behavior is simply weak, or worse teaches the wrong behavior. However, if the command and behavior with reward are timed within seconds the learning is quick and repeated easily.

Horses are just as smart about the command, behavior, and reward sequence as dogs. Otherwise how would all those movie and circus horses perform, not to mention lions, tigers, elephants, and bears? The average horse lover may walk up to a horse and give them an apple sugar, or carrot, but many horse owners don't seem to understand how to make use of the horse performing for this treat.

Part of the difference is that dogs perform on the ground whereas

horses besides performing on the ground, also carry a rider, which complicates the commands and system of rewards. The timing is still critical performance criteria as will be clarified in the following case studies about horse learning complicated tasks (Part II).

Key Points

- One of the most important and often overlooked aspects of using reward or punishing consequences is **perfect timing** that supports **perfect practice**.
- Any consequence should immediately follow behavior to be effective––this includes what are commonly called rewards, punishments, and the release of an unpleasant cue –negative reinforcers that are commonly called rider aids.
- Perfect timing is at the core of effectiveness.
- If the treat/reward is clearly presented and **timed** with the behavior a horse will learn to stand on a given cue (as other taught behaviors).
- Teaching a stand-in, such as pat-pat, is effectively used while riding.
- The careful practice method creates the actual atmosphere to produce positive horses.

Correct Longe Work

Classical longe work is evident in many European equestrian schools. The famous example is the Spanish Riding School of Austria, where students practice riding skills on a horse controlled by the riding master. I experienced these lessons both in Germany and in England. Young or inexperienced riders aren't turned loose to gallop off into the sunset, but they practice riding skills safely on an experienced horse under the control of the teacher. Many riders will longe their horse before riding, especially at competitions to ensure physical exercise and to calm an excited horse, but many riders don't consider the positive effect of using longe work to polish the skills/cues that the rider desires in the saddle: correct transitions: walk, trot, and canter.

Particularly noted during my experience while riding in several European training establishments, was the use of classical longe work not only with the horse but also for the riders. During a summer while riding at an English training establishment that trained the students in the skills necessary to pass the testing for British Horse Society (BHS), I was introduced to classical longe work for both horses and riders. Since one of the assessment skills necessary to pass the BHS certificate is to demonstrate not only the correct techniques of teaching the student to ride using longe work, but also demonstrate the ability to ride correctly without reins or stirrups.

Correct longe work is the next step to complete the basic training for the horse to ensure that they understand basic commands. These commands become the basis for future work including riding. The horse is quietly and calmly helped to learn the cues for walk, trot, and canter. This allows the horse to develop athletically without the hindrance of the rider. Large horses benefit from the longe work procedure, since it allows them to develop their muscles to support their heavy frames

Running a horse around on a normal halter is incorrect single line longeing. The objective of the longe lesson is to teach the horse to move athletically forward on the correct cues of the whip and longe line. According to Podhajshy (1976), described in his book "*The Complete Training of Horse and Rider*" correct longe work (diagrams pages 75-76), the longe line as you may see in the diagram is **not** connected under the horse's nose but importantly on top where it encourages the horse to move forward and not pull the horse to the trainer. (See above photo of Firestar correctly performing longe work).

While seemingly an unimportant point to many riders, this fine point of correct longe work is extremely important when starting a young horse. The reason why longe work often fails occurs when trainers support chasing and scaring horses to move forward and don't teach learned cues. This chasing will **not** transfer into the saddle. The rider now resorts to "kick 'em' in the belly". Certainly not the gentle method they propose. To train **positive horses**, the horse must systematically be taught cues they can learn/understand and the cues must be transferable to other horse training environments.

While your efforts might not be focused on a highly trained dressage horse, the positive aspect of longeing horses using this method provides calm easily understood taught cues. The basic training methods for any well-trained horse are the basic teachable cues:

1 Move forward on the correct cue of a sound and the pointing the longe whip— **not** chasing, throwing things at the horse, shouting at them, or kicking.

Taught Cues =Forward on Commands

2 Understand the cue of the lightly restraining longe line (the beginning of the half-halt as described in chapter seven), which teaches the horse the correct cues of transitions, which will be used in the saddle including voice commands.

The teaching of sequential cues explains that teaching horses the commands to move forward and stop is a matter of **not** running the horse and around frightening them but methodically teaching cues (pictured with using a longe whip) that are taught and understood by the horse).

The case study (Part II) of beginning groundwork with a large but very agreeable mare provides how the cues may be used. Jewel already knows the cue to come and stand in front of the trainer. Building on this cue the next sequence is for her to learn and refine the two cues: move forward and stop. All the cues are taught during groundwork and these cues are also developed to be used in the saddle. The mare already knows it's pleasurable to be with the trainer because of previous training sessions. There will be two new parts for her to learn, added to the previous cue, move forward on the voice cue and allow the whip to calmly direct the forward movement.

Three days into the lesson and the mare is moving forward several steps and stopping on voice command. The whip is carried, but it isn't used to frighten the horse. The next step will be to use the whip to point and touch.

She walks at my side and the voice cue is used with the addition of the pointing whip. Each step of walking forward on command is reinforced and based on the procedures taught in the previous lesson: Come, Stand, Walk-on, Halt.

Key Points

- Correct longe works teaches the horse correct cues needed to successfully and safely ride horses.
- Horses aren't merely run around on the longe line for exercise, but they learn important cues such as the correct canter depart.
- The trainer has the safe viewpoint to train the horse from the ground before practicing difficult skills in the saddle such as the canter depart.
- A horse that consistently learns to perform a balanced canter depart on the longe becomes easily ridden.
- Even though classical longe work is important for dressage horses, it may be used successfully for horses to be shown in many equestrian disciplines: halter classes, Western and English classes, carriage work (see the case study with Fox Part II).

Successfully Using Rider Aids

While various methods to explain the use of rewards use both food and the taught **stand-in** reward. An excellent **stand-in** reward for saddle work is the **pat-pat** that has been conditioned with a food reward. The pat-pat means something to the horse, because it has been parried with something that is understood. The stand-in sound of a clicker used for teaching horse skills on the ground has little use as soon as the rider gets into the saddle. An understanding of sounds and cues needs to become effectively used in what is traditionally called 'rider aids', and reinforced as a taught stand-in reward. There are other techniques that use the science of behavior modification and expand the methods to those techniques that are effective for the serious rider and create positive horses.

Because the constant use of primary of food rewards is unnecessary, stand-in rewards are important to teach the horse. *"In Behavior Principles"*(p.36), Ferster, Culberstson, and Boren describe using a cricket to stand for rewards. To summarize: The dog has food placed in a bowl and immediately hears the sound of the cricket. After several repetitions the sound of the cricket has become a secondary reinforcer and stands-in for food. Every time the dog hears the cricket, he receives a secondary reinforcer—the stand-in. The trainer then proceeds to teach a routine by sending the dog to perform a task such as go to a spot in the room. Each time the dog makes a move toward the desired spot the cricket is sounded, and the behavior is reinforced using the reward stand-in sound.

Several animal trainers posited if these ideas worked so well for dogs, they could be applied to horses as well. If the horse training is completed only on the ground, dog similar behavior can be taught. By not addressing the other aspects of behavioral training, clicker training is an extremely limited method for training ridden horses, because it doesn't explain the rider aid of using reins and many other rider aids. For the following example the focus will be on the rider aid using reins.

Behavior Modification for Serious Riders Aids

Having competed in national events in Europe, as a Grand Prix level rider/trainer, it is clear that the aids for a serious or casual rider demand an understanding of how these complex behaviors may be taught. This includes all the equitation disciplines that require what is explained as **rider aids** in most literature. When the rider picks up the reins, the serious rider should understand the behavior dynamics of the reins in connection to the horse that require a much different effect than explained by clicker training.

While there are various aspects to riding, an explanation of rider aids should be addressed. The simple fact is: All riders include some mild reminder to the horse, which is a command, cue, or called 'rider aids'. No matter what your riding discipline, there is an important overlooked aspect of these 'riders aids'. Before beginning describing the scientific facts that operate ridden horse behavior—rider aids, the following is important:

1. Teaching any complicated series of behaviors means the animal understands what is asked and has the skills to perform those tasks. This is the teaching technique that is effectively used to teach anyone difficult tasks including, flying airplanes, teaching reading to young children, performing dance steps......etc.
2. A simple description of the rider rein aid is: The rider gives the cue and as soon as the horse responds, the mildly asking aid is stopped upon the correct horse response.

Unfortunately, most rider aids could be described as mildly unpleasant, but the knowledgeable rider who understands how rider aids function can be taught to make them no more than a small nudge. My grand prix horses all performed flying change with only a slight unperceivable change in cues.

The renowned German Olympic trainer, Harry Bolt (1978), exemplifies perfect rider aids in his beautiful pictorial book *Das Dressur Pferd (The Dressage Horse)*. This famous book shows photos of every stride for several dressage exercises; it is hard to see any change in his position. Most expert riders intuitively learn that the timing of these mildly unpleasant rider aids to be effective, are only effective when very carefully used and stopped **immediately** upon performed behavior.

The horse contributes to or teaches the rider as Podhajsky (1969), writes in his book *My Horses My Teachers*. "Although they had no faculty of speech, they taught me more than many humans did. Therefore I feel that I should relate my experiences with my horses for the sake and benefit of future generations of horses and riders" (p. 3). As an expert rider trains and rides, they are aware of their rider aids in relationship to horse performance and seek to repeat quiet aids and release uncomfortable cues immediately. Most accomplished riding teachers focus their students on quiet horse commands even if they don't explain the details of the behavioral method underlying why the command is effective — or not. The rider by understanding the behavioral underpinnings has an advantage in understanding how to create and fix rider aids—especially when they don't work. Instead of the rider becoming increasingly forceful, they reevaluate the cause and effect of the rider aid.

Explanation of Rider Aids

What is the significance of the negative reinforcer to the rider aid of using reins?

Even though the words seem to be a contradiction in meaning, a simple way to describe a negative reinforcer could be translated into a mildly unpleasant cue that when stopped encourages, increases, or rewards the behavior that follows the mildly unpleasant cue. An uncomplicated way to describe this concept is the removal of uncomfortable shoes, or a tight belt…the immediate results is relief. The mildly unpleasant cue, if it is to be effective, should produce immediate results and increase the following desired behavior. This is important to understand, because if the mildly unpleasant cue connected with what is called a rider aid doesn't produce the desired behavior, the cue or desired behavior is not correct.

There are several possibilities for a stand-in reinforcer.

"For the most part it is unnecessary to use only
one cue or secondary reinforcer for horses because they
aren't "sent" to a spot. Described in the chapter; Review

Rider Aids and Devices, horses are taught a variety of routines and are more successfully reinforced by using the various objects connected with each task as the cue or secondary reinforcer —no need for a clicker gadget" (Dammier, 2001, p. 144).

The scientific explanation for a <u>Negative Reinforcer</u> is : (Dammier 2001, p. 126).

Table 8 Negative Reinforcer

Stimulus signal or cue	Behavior	Consequence
Reins in contact with the horse's mouth	The horse yields and lightens contact	Reins release pressure/contact to the horse's mouth

Summary: Often this example of the rider aid fails because the rider does not release the pressure of the reins immediately after the horse yields. Sometimes the rider lacks basic riding skills allowing the hands to be steady and used independently of the seat. Balancing the rider's position using the reins often causes the horse to raise the head to protect against the harsh use of hands. The horse eventually stiffens against the unyielding pressure and fails to move in the energetic, athletic manner of the free horse.

Negative reinforcers or mildly unpleasant cues called **rider aids**, are part of the rider in the saddle for any equine discipline. Understanding how they function is important in creating the easy-going calm relationship we want with **positive horses.**

Rider Rein Aids -The Secret of Using a Half-Halt

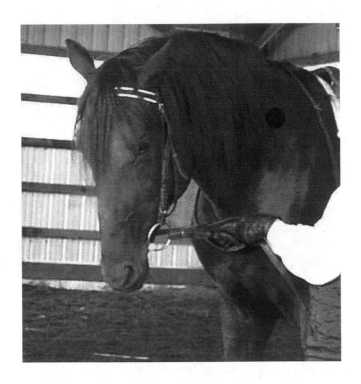

An important rein aid is described as a half-halt. The **rider aid** or a negative reinforcer called a **half-halt**, is a basic cue used in several equestrian disciplines, but is especially important in the discipline of dressage. The **half-halt** is the basis for much horse training and the means to communicate. Since much of this communication is through signals given through the reins of a bridle or lines that are connected to a halter, it's important that the communication gives clear directions. This means the horse has been carefully taught these **rein aids** and understands what behaviors are to be performed. Even though rider aids may be performed through force, horses will perform a better through the method of learned cues. Most horses are fairly cooperative when systematically taught cues connected to performance.

As discussed in the last chapter emphasizing perfect practice and perfect timing, the half-halt when taught correctly may have a profound influence on creating a positive horse. According to the famous director of the Spanish Riding School of Vienna, home of the Lipizzaner horses, Alois Podhajsky, the half-halt is the foundation of horse training. Podhajsky (1965) in his book *The Complete Training of Horse and rider* states, "The half-halt may be described as a "call to attention' to prepare the horse for the next command of the rider" (p. 40). Before the half-halt is taught under rider, it is taught during the first lessons on the longe line, which is why beginning correct longe work is extremely important.

If we use Podhajsky's description of a basic important rider aid and further describe the action in terms of a negative reinforcer tool, the precise implementation or perfect timing becomes important to understand how this rider aid functions. Podhajsky (1974), cautions the rider in the use of the rider aid. "The rein action should not degenerate into a steady pull" (p.79). In his book *The Riding Teacher* he adds an important part to his clarification that the incorrect use of the rider aid would cause the horse to pull on the reins rather than performing the correct behavior of giving to the reins. Describing Podhajsky's explanation of the half-halt in terms of a negative reinforcer, this steady pull is unsuccessful in gaining cooperation and athletic lightness from the horse, because the steady pull never stops the unpleasant part of the command. It's the equivalent of nagging. Where as if the command is eased the horse understands the connection to becoming cooperative. Here's how the cue may look behaviorally outlined:

Table 9 Half-Halt

Cue	Behavior	Consequence
Depending on the rider discipline and how the rider handles the reins: 1 - Closes the fingers squeezing them on the rein * 2 - The rider takes slight tension on the reins	The horse upon the rider giving the appropriate cue relaxes and eases giving to the tension and depending on the strength of the cue makes a transition to another gait and or lightens the contact with the horse immediately upon correct performance.	For this cue to become as effective the rider must ease the tension to make clear to the horse that the desired behavior has been performed.

* To test this effect, take one of your reins and have someone hold one end of the rein and take the other correctly in your hand with the rein fully in the hand with your thumb facing up. Squeeze the fingers and watch the change in the rein. For a dressage rider contact, this slight aid encourages the horse to be light in the cooperative effort.

Importance of Negative Reinforcer

So how does this important rider tool translate in the concept of the negative reinforcer? The rider needs to develop other stand-in reinforcers. Here's where those sound, pat-pat and stand-in that were previously taught with food cues become real rewards. All the previous work taught on the ground such as: come, stand, walk-on, and halt continue to be used into the saddle. This is a stairway of learned skills. Since an important part of the negative reinforcer is stopping the mildly unpleasant command exactly upon the desired behavior performed by the horse, the timing is critical for success. Using the rider aid example of a half-halt, which is used in equestrian disciplines, the explanation of the negative reinforcer or the mildly uncomfortable cue is important. Whether the horse training is tugging on a line or a rein the behavioral description is the same, this is a mildly unpleasant cue.

Negative reinforcers are not really negative if understood. They can be made positive is by understanding how the cue is taught. In chapter four of Behavior Modification for Horses (Dammier, 2019), I list three headings about negative reinforcers: *Not Really Negative, Negative Reinforcers as Useful Training Tools, and Negative Reinforcers with Negative Results.* There are several important parts that are summarized and should be remembered for the use of reins:

Table 10 Negative Reinforcement – Use of Reins
(Dammier, 2001, p. 33)

Cue	Behavior	Consequence
Visual cue – sound, touch, sight	An action that stops	An effect or actions — pressure on the horse's mouth
Reins in contact with the horse's mouth	The horse reduces movement	Reins apply pressure the mouth and release as soon as the horse performs

1. Rider aids are mildly unpleasant cues that need to be released immediately as soon as the horse performs.
2. Easy tasks are taught before more difficult ones.
3. Primary reinforcers (food rewards) are taught with secondary reinforcers (stand-in) that are taught to substitute for the tangible rewards. Remember that if you give a treat at the same time you 'pat-pat' a horse the pat-pat will become a stand-in.

4. Many of the cues used with horses are mildly unpleasant – there isn't anyway to say that having someone even lightly tugging on you is okay.

5. However, there is a positive aspect to this rider aid and that is that positive quick timing of the release, which produces the positive horse.

Equestrian Literature

Horse Training Promoted In Literature

The following chapter is a survey of the common horse training material available that range from general information, care of pet horses, and instruction of various riding disciplines. This literature survey provides the reader with reasons explained by several researchers for why positive reward training isn't commonly used by horse trainers. If the literature is critically analyzed, the potential horse trainer may better understand the basic principles that underline the skill training necessary for any animal. With over a hundred years of educational material, there is much accurate fact-based horse information, but it rarely reaches the general public. There are several reasons:

1. Publishers don't think this literature will sell.
2. The material publishes may submit although factual, doesn't give specific application.
3. The mass media hype promotes what is thought to be Hollywood type presentable books and actually censors what they consider not 'catchy' enough.
4. The information has to be so simple that the average person is attracted in less than thirty seconds.
5. The material must have a catchy slogan or tagline —this doesn't necessarily mean that it has content.
6. So 'instant results' and 'new training gadgets' sell training.

Most of the general information books about horse and care of pets encounter little difficulties in providing accurate factual material. The inadequacies fall mainly in the training literature. While many animals share some of the same behavioral responses, (species specific behavior) horses are a unique category of behavior, because they not only perform on the ground, but also perform other disciplines such as jumping, racing, equitation, dressage, and driving with carriages to name a few.

Beautiful pictures of horses are found in the book *Equus: The Creation of a Horse.* Vavra (1977), has photographed horses in breathtaking backgrounds. This quintessential coffee table book invites endless viewing for a horse lover. The frolicking two white stallions on pages 142-145 prance free on a beach in Fuentebravia, Spain. This book is a personal memoir, because I was there during the photography of the free running stallions and knew several of the horses during the time I lived in Spain. These two stallions had been trained, as others in the Domeque equestrian school, by a Portuguese trainer. Besides the exquisite photographs, are descriptions and behavior comments for each horse photo in the book's supplement.

An example of the equine books concerned with breeding is seen in the above photo. Firefox, a black stallion bred from a Russian Orlov Rostopchin stallion and a German Trakehner mare, is reading about his mare's breed in *The Ultimate Horse Book*. The book is described for those who love horses and has pictures and descriptions of many popular horse breeds. While a love for horses is important, the next subject of concern is how they will be trained.

Much of the horse literature seeks to apply other animal training such as dogs and dolphins to horses. Several of the scientific methods of reinforcement may limitedly be applied. The difficulty in applying these behavioral techniques is that these animals naturally have other environments. For example dogs are trained on the ground to respond to different cues so a sound gadget works well because the trainer is also on the ground. Horses however, have their own unique instincts and behavior characteristics. Eventually the trainer will athletically ride from a saddle or drive in a carriage. To begin teaching cues with a sound gadget is not practical for future training, so the cues must be established with that in mind.

Unfortunately to a large extent, horse training hype consists of using the jargon from humanistic psychology and lacks any specifics about how both animals and humans learn new behavior. Humanistic psychology has much to offer humans for quality of life, but it is based on the use of language between the therapist and the client. Nonverbal behavior may influence both animals and humans, but horses base their reaction on previous learned observable cues. To make these desired cues securely learned, a conscientious effort to repeat a sequential lesson must be followed by the trainer. Most of the predominant horse training literature is based on self-proclaimed experts who have teams of marketing experts to write their copy. The marketing copy is produced to sell books and has little practical use for training application. Many horse trainers describe behavioral horse training and use appropriate sounding words from the field of ethology- the study of animal genetics and behavior.

There are several highly qualified equestrian experts who have shared their views about the worth of the predominant horse literature. The irritation among several not only qualified equestrians but highly educated credentialed researchers, are the lack of any factual descriptions about horse training. According to Jean Claude Barrey, who is a French ethologist, horseman, and teacher, he is concerned that the practice of horse whispering promotes fantasies rather than facts. He criticizes the model that chases horses and ignores the fear factor in making the horse submit to the trainers, because the horse has no choice. Barrey (n.d.) states that the focus is media attention and producing rapid results.

According to Andy Beck from the *White Horse Farm Equine Ethology Project in Northland/New Zealand* (n.d.), "Horses that have already been well socialized to people become extremely confused by being driven away. The horse has no idea why it is harried and is most likely to experience the method as unpredictable aggression—the last thing a good trainer wants a horse to experience (p.1)."

An example of this type of unpredictable aggression by the trainer and the horse response is illustrated in Part II. Firefox from the time he was 3-months-old was consistently trained to the understandable basic clear cues: come, stand, walk forward, and halt. Horses are very consistent in their behavior when a predicable procedure is followed. This explains why Fox, as he is called, is always so easy to work with and extremely calm until this 5-second mistake of a 'yahoo' trainer, to all of our shock, had him running backwards.

Rather than chasing the horse and forcing them by blocking them, a horse may be taught in about 5-minutes to come to the trainer and stand – at liberty – free —with no ropes around the neck using positive reinforcements/rewards paired with the cue to stand. These trainers talk about using desensitization, a word snatched from psychology books. Actually the concept was researched by Watson 1920 and later in 1950 by the scientist Wolpe, who worked with human patients in a 3-step fear reducing method that had the patient visualize the source of the fear in a non-threatening environment. However, this concept has little to do with horses in the context of chasing a horse, rather the over exposure of the item of the chasing rope may cause the horse to learn the item as a fear producing cue. Rather than desensitizing, the trainer with a rope in hand may have become a cue for an unpleasant happening. In the future, every time the horse has a rope pulling on the neck he will run away. As we witnessed with Fox, this happened very quickly but with the immediate stopping of this lesson everything continued as normal. If horses have a solid positive training foundation, often an isolated traumatic occurrence is overshadowed and quickly forgotten. We immediately took over the lesson and Fox recognized his normal trainers who gave the 'stand command', which Fox instantly performed. Imagine a horse running backwards and within seconds standing quietly at attention because of a practiced cue.

A research project that paralleled Fox's experience, analyzed several reported nonviolent methods. The demonstration of an Arab horse being asked to stand was repeatedly and sharply pulled by the lead line. While probably not causing much pain, the demonstration of natural horsemanship was described as nonviolent (Muller, Crzanowska, & Pisula).

Horses that have been traumatized by round-pen training and the methods of chasing them is providing explanations for using alternative methods. An article published by Cavallo Magazine (2003), provided a discussion about the reasons that this type of training may fail. There are indications that these methods often encounter complication or even failure due to an element of force that is completely denied by the trainers. A horse isn't really free if someone is chasing him.

Regrettably most of the equestrian literature that is promoted in the mass media is based what can be quickly sold to the horse trainer. The common theme of "natural" and "mysterious" are promoted in an attempt to lure horse owners into thinking that horse education is a quick undertaking. Loosely defined terms taken from management and psychology terms are popularized and used to support the academic impression. Statements such as:

- "You have to teach your horse to respect you."
- "You have to show your horse you're the alpha member."
- "You have to teach them who's boss

The inaccurate use of popularized management and psychology terms tell the trainer absolutely nothing about the specific actions/behaviors needed to train a horse. Most of these popularized terms sound good and are a mixture of media marketing sales techniques… what will catch on and sell. It's disheartening to know that there is an abundance of excellent research from both and the educational and psychological perspective that never reaches the popular equestrian audience. The problem is that the ideas about how animals learn aren't easily and accurately explained.

Material from learning theory helps explain the precise connection between what happens before and after any behavior. Simple. It's a matter of self-training to analyze a cause and effect relationship. There should be more attempts to connect valuable learning theory with practical application, but unfortunately this isn't the focus of the popular equestrian media. The trend in the current media is that whatever sells get promoted.

With the added tendency for quick fixes for everything and "it has to feel good" attitude, there is a lack of substance in the promoted animal training ideas. The general equestrian population is sold gimmicks because of the lack of critical thinking on the part of the reader.

Key Points

- There are a many types of equestrian books to motivate horse lovers.
- Many animals share some of the same behavioral responses, but horses are a unique category of behavior because they not only perform on the ground, but also perform other disciplines such as jumping, racing, equitation, dressage, and driving with carriages to name a few.
- The unique aspect behavior of horses should be considered in training literature.
- Horse literature should be scrutinized for logical sequence for training horse behavior—not fast techniques. Animals similar

to humans need numerous repetitions over several days to perform difficult skills.

- Use of popularized management and psychology terms tell the trainer absolutely nothing about the specific actions/behaviors needed to train a horse.

Part II

1. Using Basic Skills to Train for Driving a Cart
2. Firestar and the "Yahoo"- Fixing Negative Behavior
3. Jewel Beginning Lessons: Come, Stand, Walk on, and Halt
4. Story of Great Dane Allie- Teaching a Safety Cue

Benefits of Working With Horses and Carts

The following training case study is to demonstrate that horses with correct basic skills have potential versatility depending on the quality of past training and each horse's individual talents. Each horse from an early age demonstrates natural tendencies toward learning. Any classroom teacher can tell you this simple fact, which is why standard education— one size – fits all is nonsensical. With horses the same follows in that each horse should be considered for the steps in learning.

Presently on the farm there are three middle-aged horses all from the same mare, but each one demonstrates many of her characteristics but differences in sensitivity. The three horses are an interesting case study, because they were all born on the farm and trained for dressage work by me. Two of the horses, now geldings, were stallions until very late. The only reason they were gelded was because of the dwindling horse industry and the farm's logistics. Fox was more energetic and interested in the other horses compared to his half-brother Star. When Star walked past the other horses on his way for training in the arena he never called whereas, Fox would begin calling loudly. Anyone visiting a baby nursery may view several children crying at the top of their lungs, some sleeping peacefully, and still others happily looking around. Each brings natural aspects of hereditary and experience.

As a consideration for a likely carriage horse, Star would have made the better candidate compared to the energetic Fox. However, Fox is extremely smart and as dog trainers walk into a kennel and pick those dogs easiest to train, Fox made the grade because he learned the 'stand cue' perfectly. Not only would he stand on cue, but he would pose at attention and stay as if a statue. One of the necessary traits for a carriage horse is to stand quietly. This has made all the steps of introducing the training cart easy. The stand cue also focuses him on the positive relation of the trainer commands.

Potential for More Interest in Driving

In recent years there are more retired and potential new equestrians while wanting to be part of the horsey scene who may not have the athletic ability required to ride.

Even those equestrians that will be able to mount and ride horses will greatly benefit from driving a horse and cart. The sports industry has taken more interest in a population that is not interested in competing but rather the fun part of being close with animals.

While studying dressage in Europe, I was exposed to the benefit of carriage work frequently, because almost every riding school performed work with horses and carriages. It's not only a custom but also an easy method of training riders.

Fox lessons: Beginning Work With a Carriage/ Training Cart

Summary: Fox has excellent beginning work for correct longe work, under saddle, and classical long reining. He has all the basic skills that should make him an outstanding horse for carriage work. One part necessary for carriage horses is to stand quietly with the carriage. Using the 'stand cue', Fox already stands quietly at liberty for harnessing and saddling, blanketing, and cleaning hoofs. This skill has made it easy to quickly finish time taking routines— walk into the stall, give the command to stand and proceed with tasks.

Friday

Began to put Fox back in work. It should never be assumed that the horse remembers all lessons; review is a safe procedure.

- Began with fifteen minutes with longe line work using the bridle he wears while ridden.
- Fox always does well on the longe so this is to start him back into work, after a short several week pause because of bad weather.
- The first days' work is to review walk, trot, canter cues on the longe line following all the commands including 'walk on' and halt. It is always interesting that horses started correctly remember correct work even with a break in training.

Saturday

- Continued the previous day work and added additional time to trot and canter.
- Practiced walk on and halt while on the longe but also reviewed walking along side him in preparation for the assistant.

Sunday

- Fox has had both a vaulting surcingle and a saddle on his back. Today I put only the surcingle part of the driving equipment, with the addition of the tail section called a crupper, which helps keep the harnessing in place. The crupper is a piece of harness that goes around the tail and can sometimes be an annoyance. This went well and he didn't seem to mind the crupper at the walk and trot. At the canter he noticed a bit and made two steps noticing the tension on his tail. Otherwise everything went fine.
- Walk, trot, and canter practice and leading at the shoulder with commands to walk on and halt. It should never be assumed that small changes don't upset the horse or disturb confidence. It is prudent to proceed with small steps. Small mistakes may be corrected when built on substantial quality work. The trainer may easily step back to a successful lesson for review before proceeding to the new skill.

Monday

- First day with the surcingle and crupper part of the driving equipment.
- Training a new assistant that has some English riding experience but specifically unknown. Past experience has helped me understand that it is never good to assume anything about someone's horse training experience.
- Fox stood on command at liberty in his stall while being outfitted. Walked him to the arena and demonstrated the command to walk on and halt with the trainer correctly standing at the shoulder.
- Proceeded to command Fox forward to walk on in a large circle gave the commands to walk, trot, and canter on both reins. The assistant took the longe line and whip and proceeded to walk around the arena performing walk-on and halt commands.
- These commands are needed so that the assistant may walk the horse safely while the trainer begins training the horse to accept the cart being walked behind and eventually pulling the cart in future lessons.
- The assistant walked correctly at the horse's shoulder but by using the right hand nearest the horse to hold the longe line, and the left hand furthest from the horse for the whip. The horse was being drawn into the assistant rather than allowing the horse to walk a straight line. The correct in-hand work position is the line in the left with the whip next to the horse to encourage the driving aid of walking forward.

Tuesday

- Longed Fox: Walk, trot, and canter using the vaulting surcingle.
- Practiced walking in hand to the command walk on and halt for the practice we need for the cart work. Put the reins through the surcingle for long rein practice. It was a good review for driving

practice. This was a long rein review day. This is the long rein work that is not what is commonly called driving which entails risk to the trainer on the ground. The classical long rein work that Fox was taught was prefaced on correct longe work.

- Classical long rein works allows the horse to be given command as if ridden. The advantage is being able to see the quality of the rider aids.

1. Correct longe work: walk, trot, canter
2. The next step to begin safe long rein work to introduce the second rein with the trainer in a safe position
3. The trainer based on the horse's understanding of the cues to walk-on and halt, introduces the second rein. A clear detailed description of classical long rein training is found in both the Heinrich and Stanier books.
4. Stanier (2001), in her classic book about long reining, explains, "The idea of schooling is to produce a well-balanced supple horse… Long reining is a medium through which the ridden horse can be produced, not an end in itself (xv).

Wednesday

- Repeated the previous day longe lesson walk, trot, and canter.
- The goal is that the horse habitually preforms the cues of walk, trot, and canter.
- Worked with the assistant on the longe line work so she is confident in handling Fox especially in the event of a mistake. The assistant practiced without my presence and gave the commands to walk-on and halt.
- Again we walked around the edge of the arena with cart controlled by me several paces behind fox. We made several walk on and stop. The focus is to have Fox become accustomed to someone/something behind him.

- Carriage work is several months of successful skills of not only attaching a cart. Fox has been long reined for the preliminary work for being ridden. He has been trained to accept the trainer walking to his hindquarter and crossing behind with the long reins over his back.
- Had the assistant longe Fox to have the feel of the longe line and use of driving commands. Worked with the assistant on the circle with me giving commands. Practiced the commands walk, trot, and canter with me as the driving assistant and she had control of the main longe line.
- She practiced taking Fox along the wall to practice walk and halt. She did very well and this was a confidence building sessions so she has a chance to direct Fox by herself.
- This went so well we brought the cart up for Fox to see and walked the cart behind while the assistant led him along the arena wall. The commands for stop and walk on were given.
- The cart was brought up a little closer even slightly brushing Fox's side with the tracer. We rewarded Fox and took him back to his stall, unharnessed, and gave him his midday meal.

Thursday

- The lesson begins with the longe lesson of walk, trot, and canter. This establishes work that has been successfully completed. It may seem unnecessary, but it's a method of having the horse perform skills correctly even though they may not be directly related to the present lesson it's important to constantly build on pervious taught and learned skills.
- The assistant now takes control of the longe lesson. At the end of the right rein circle Fox turned slightly into the circle instead of halting squarely on the circle. This is a perfect opportunity to discuss positive corrections. Instead of jolting the longe line to reprimand him, we quietly walked up to Fox, repositioned him, and began the lesson on the circle.

- Fox was totally quiet and this was a perfect opportunity about the lesson of correction: there are no perfect horses or trainers, but **successful correction**. Much the way we would correct a young child learning to read— the correct response is quietly given and practiced.
- The horse often doesn't connect the reprimand with the behavior—practicing the correct behavior is effective learning creating the positive horse.
- Quiet corrections practice the correct response.
- It was time to practice with the cart walking behind with the assistant giving the walk on and stop commands. We halted. Fox stood perfectly. The assistant stood and Fox was rewarded for standing.
- The cart now was slowly brought closer to the position where it would be correctly attached to the tracers. Fox continued to stand perfectly still as he could see the tracers, and they slightly brushed his side. He looked but stood in his perfect halt confidently waiting for the assistant to reward him with a carrot exactly timed with the behavior of standing perfectly still.
- Fox turned to see if his reward was forthcoming, I coached the assistant to wait until he was not looking at her and in the halt stance. This is **very** important —rewards must be perfectly timed as explained in the chapter about timing consequences. Fox stayed perfectly for about 3 minutes. We were just thrilled at this moment,
- The cart was backed away and Fox walked back to his stall for the midday meal. Fox is demonstrating that he understands and is confident in the commands.

Important to the safety of the training session with the cart is:

1. Having the trained assistant.
2. Not prematurely attaching a potentially dangerous cart before Fox has time to practice and build his confidence.

Friday

- Began the lesson with the walk, trot, and canter lesson.
- The assistant is taking more responsibility as it's important her to have confidence in the ability to handle the horse. Horses also recognize people known to them.
- Classical longe work is <u>not</u> merely running the horse around by chasing him with a rope or even on a line.
- It's the correct athletic training that teaches the horse the correct effect of the rider rein and driving aids. It's the same touch that the rider uses in the saddle and allows communication with the horse. It's important for the assistance to be well-acquainted with Fox, because we're adding new skills that are dependent on his confidence.
- We continued with the previous day's work of having the assistant walk Fox at the edge of the arena giving the commands to walk on and halt.
- The cart was then walked slightly behind him repeating the walk-on and halt commands. Fox could hear the cart behind him and was totally concentrating on the assistant's commands.
- Fox was halted as the previous day and the cart brought up to the correct position where it was going to be attached to the surcingle. Fox stood perfectly still and the assistant rewarded him for standing on command.
- We then asked fox to take several steps forward and halt with the cart in the close position. The tracers are under the surcingle and not attached in case Fox might suddenly be afraid. If this occurred the assistant would move fox ahead and I would take the cart backwards from the close position. Fox can see the end of the tracers and he's totally unconcerned.
- We still aren't going to attach the cart until we have several days of totally calm behavior. It would ruin any possibility of successfully teaching Fox to drive if the cart frightened him.

Even though a well-known trainer demonstrated running a horse around, putting on a saddle and rider in 30 minutes, this is a disaster waiting to happen. Patient small increments of skills promote consistent more permanent learning. The horse in this demo ran around bucking when the saddle was first put on. They're lucky that this didn't occur with the rider. Sequential cinching would have prevented this error, but of course the 30 minutes would have been used up.

At a famous riding establishment in Portugal, over a hundred young stallions were started and not one stallion ever bucked during the stage of beginning saddling and riding, but these horses weren't rushed through in 30 minutes, but rather quietly and patiently worked through longeing, saddling, and rider mounting over several days depending on the horse. Of course this establishment was training horse athletics for exceptional skills and didn't want to risk mistakes that would hinder progress and reliability. Unfortunately horses remember both good and bad skills, and bad skills are almost impossible to change without great difficulty. Best to take a little more time than risk mistakes; enough happen randomly.

One technique is to cinch sequentially. Even though Fox is totally trained under saddle we didn't assume any of the skills and verified each step. The carriage surcingle was not totally tensioned for these lessons and will progressively tightened as we have start to have Fox pull the cart.

Saturday

The plan was an easy day for the horses getting turned out and only maintenance work with Fox to keep the lessons. There is research that supports many sequential lessons of less time yield greater success than few lessons of greater periods of practice. Perfect practice makes perfect; restraining the tendency to one more repetition. Better to end on the correct performance, leaving that the last behavior practiced.

Today working alone on the farm started wrong when I unknowingly left the stall unlatched to go and retrieve an additional item. All the horses are well-behaved in that an open door doesn't mean bolt and run out but a wide open door after time invites curiosity. Not realizing the door didn't latch, I wasn't in a hurry only to walk across the courtyard and see Fox looking out his open door and taking a few steps to see what grass he could find. Amazing how the mare way in the front somehow knew that Fox was quietly walking around the courtyard and suddenly started to call to him. It is always amazing how the taught 'safety cue' works. I walked up to Fox gave him to signal to come. He immediately came and we walked back to his stall.

- Since the day's lesson had begun with some excitement, I decided to practice his normal longe routine of walk, trot and canter to end on a positive note. Fox performed as normal.
- The cart was sitting in the arena so I walked Fox over in front of the cart with the tracers resting on the ground. I walked Fox one step forward and since he knows how to walk backward (The cue is to walk was given and the half-halt to make the walk move backwards) I asked for 1-step backwards. Fox walked backwards and stood between the tracers. I asked him to walk forward and then one step backwards. He walked calmly and straight backwards between the tracers. We ended on this positive note and went back to his stall for lunch.

Note – Read chapter about behaviorally teaching the half-halt.

Sunday-Day off

Monday

- Performed his normal walk, trot and canter lesson.
- Coached the assistant to lightly handle the longe line and coordinate the longe whip. It is important to note conflicting or contradicting the rein effect of the longe line, while the driving the horse with the longe whip demands concentration of the trainer. It's a fine coordination of small directions that don't override the other command of moving forward.

- We again had the assistant walk around the arena practicing the walk and halt command.
- Once again brought the cart into the position of being connected, but rather than buckling the tracer to the surcingle, I again held a leather strap that could be released if Fox was uncertain.
- Again we walked with cart in place 2-steps and halted. On the long wall of the arena, we repeated 2-steps and halt. When halted he stood perfectly still. We rewarded Fox and removed the cart.
- Return to the stall for lunch.

Tuesday

- Began the longe lesson again demonstrated the importance of positioning the trainer correctly. If the trainer stands slightly in front of the horse and waves the whip at the horse's side, the horse will merely turn inward. The correct position is at the horse's side, parallel to the horse, commanding the horse to walk on. Fox is very easily longed, so he is a good candidate for the assistant to learn the correct longeing procedures.
- This part of the lesson went easier for the assistant as she is more confident with the longe aids. As many riders, she had not a clear understanding of the benefit of correct longe work. She was amazed how easily Fox was to handle compared to her horses.
- She then preceded the 'walk on' and 'halt' exercise.
- Again we brought the cart into the correct the position.
- The cart was held in place by holding a leather strap to connect the tracers with the surcingle so Fox could feel the cart behind him. I continue to hold some of the weight of the cart, which is extremely light.
- The commands were repeated: 'walk on' and 'halt' along the long wall of the arena. We arrived to the short end of the arena only to find that the cart didn't quite follow Fox evenly because

of being held only one side of the cart. The cart slightly bumped Fox and even though Fox noticed, he only tried to move away from the right side of the tracers (I'm standing on the left). Fox kept walking forward. I am pleased that Fox is so easy-going, even with small mistakes.

- He's very calm and this is and an example of how the **trainers also become a positive cue**. We move to the long wall to make sure the cart is straight and continue taking walk on and halt commands with the cart held in place by me.
- We halt —giving Fox his carrot reward, release the cart, and walk him back to his stall for a well-earned lunch. Fox does understand that at the end of his lessons he gets lunch, because he takes a drink and then walks to wait at his dish.

Wednesday-Fox Gets a Pasture Day

Thursday

- Practice longe lesson walk, trot, and canter.
- The assistance needed a little coaching at the beginning, but she easily takes over when the horse is in balanced on the circle. The assistant needs coaching that the longe line has a fine control through a gentle consistent aid that way the reins will be handled riding. The aids are small cues not a big pull.
- By keeping the same lesson plan, but adding small skills we are successfully completing the bigger goal of having Fox independently pull the cart. At this point it would be easy to rush to the finish carriage work and even though all skills appear to be in place. This would be a mistake to risk Fox's confidence in a new potentially worrisome concept of having a 'thing' follow him around.
- As preparing for any new potentially hazardous skill, it's better to be over practiced. Similar to preparing to solo fly a small

plane, it's better to over practice before going solo; there is more confidence in having more practice; a good risk management practice.

- The assistant takes Fox solo for the 'walk on' and 'halt' practice while walking around the arena. It's important that Fox has confidence in the assistant since he sees her standing alongside him by his shoulder/head. I notice that he looks at her and she has rewarded him with carrots, so Fox additionally recognizes her as something pleasant. Remember the trainer additionally becomes paired with positive events and becomes a stand-in.

- It is almost impossible for the horse not to be pressured by the tracers or occasionally lightly bumped — it's part of an important skill lesson that takes time.

- In today's session we proceeded to bring the cart up and I held it with the quick release strap. We now went along the long wall walking and stopping but when we came to the short wall the cart didn't turn following Fox, because it wasn't attached on the right side which would have kept the cart straight. When we walked into the corner the tracer pressed Fox on the right. He stopped on command and we immediately released the cart and walked him to the long wall and continued after we had the cart straight.

- Very important to have a trained assistant with beginning work to ensure horse confidence.

- We are so happy about the way Fox reacted because of his previous positive experience with the cart. The reason we haven't buckled the cart to the surcingle is the risk safety factor of being able to immediately release the cart in the event that Fox might startle. The important skill at this stage is that Fox has confidence in the cart following behind him. We are very pleased with the results.

- This is the assistant's first time teaching a horse to correctly lead, perform on the longe line, and work with a horse being introduced to a carriage.

Friday

- Today began with the warm-up longe lesson of walk, trot, and canter and halt quietly.

- This is an excellent starting point because it starts the lessons with the skills that Fox performs consistently. It's the basis for all the following work. It also allows the foundation that if any of the new lessons are unsuccessful, the basic work may always be performed so to end a lesson on a successful note if the lesson plan is not completed.

- The next step is for the assistance to walk Fox around the arena asking him to walk on and halt. Since the assistant is in control of the commands of the cart work at this stage, it's exactly important that Fox has confidence in her ability to give commands.

- The third step now is walking with the cart behind Fox in the position where it will be attached. The cart is still **not** attached but has been held by the trainer who walks along side Fox holding the tracer.

- Since our lesson objective is to now have the cart being pulled by Fox we have the leather loops that will eventually be attached to the cart in place. The tracers on both sides are slipped through the loop but NOT attached to the cart. Even though Fox has made total progress to the work so far we do not want to take the chance to precipitously attaching the leather loop to the cart.

- Presently I can easily slip the tracers out the loop and let the assistant walk away from the cart. This solution of slipping the tracers through both sides would make the cart travel easily around the arena. The cart is so light; it's a perfect safe training carriage. We halt the cart and slip the cart into position on both sides.

- The assistant starts Fox walking. He is now actually pulling the cart and he can feel the occasional pressure of the tracers. This moment is **very** important so that the horse isn't frightened. This is why we are repeating this part of the lesson slowly with the ability to pull the cart away. Fox now walks a few steps and halts. We can see he's noticed the slight difference with the tracers on both sides. He's actually pulling the cart without the chest harness, which is not needed right now— no one is in the cart. When he halts we watch his response. He's given a carrot reward. We walk on several steps and halt.

- At the next command, Fox is a little hesitant to walk on but he's so accustomed to the assistant it's only a moment of hesitation and he listens to her command 'walk on'. Now for the rest of the arena he's walking his normal pace and has no hesitation. We let him continue to walk until all the way around the arena. Fox is totally confident in this new endeavor.
- Needless to say we're ecstatic. This is 2-weeks of consistent careful lessons of skills built on a safe plan.

Sunday

Today is a unique opportunity to have the observation of my farrier who actually does by his presence calms the horses. Steve like a few of the excellent farriers, is sensitive to the horse and its balance. Think about if you had to stand on one leg balanced with someone pushing on you.

When the mare Firebird, a large Hungarian was very young, Steve was recuperating from being ill and we had a substitute farrier. The filly had been wonderful with her feet being trimmed, but Steve was attentive to how long she could balance. Folks just assume the horse can stand forever on three legs and not lose balance. Even though I explained that the filly was well-behaved but she didn't' have more than 2 times with doing hoof trims. She was very good at picking up her feet on cue during daily cleaning. Everything was going smoothly with the new chap until he took her back leg and pulled it up and way away from her body. Just as I could see she was going to lose her balance and say something, he grabbed her hoof as she shifted her weight and roughly pulled her leg.

Since she couldn't stay on her feet, she promptly pushed him away to prevent herself from falling over; because he refused to let go of her hoof, thinking he would teach her a lesson, the hoof grazed his arm. Well, I apologized for the filly even though it wasn't her fault. We were all relieved when Steve was well enough to return, because I certainly wasn't going to risk this chap with the other two young stallions because they were so well-behaved; didn't need them learning bad habits. We delayed trimming their feet.

Unnecessary to say that Steve has never had any of the then youngsters behave poorly. In all the years that Steve has trimmed their feet, it was only once in a great while one of them might be a little more restless. He always anticipates what they need so they never try to take the hoof away from being held.

I wasn't going to do a cart lesson alone with Fox so I was pleased that my farrier had time to observe and be the cart safety guide. We're still not attaching the tracers but merely slipping the pole through the strap in case we might need to release the cart. I now was the command giver at Fox's shoulder while Steve walked behind me with his hand on the tracer shaft. After I did the short longe warm-up we brought Fox up to the cart. Even thought Steve has known Fox from the time he was young he hadn't actually seen him work. He knew how well he stands quietly for trimming.

Fox stood rock still until I gave him the command to walk on. It was going to well and we walked halfway around the arena before I gave him the command to halt. We continued walking easily and at a normal walk with no hesitations. We walked around the arena again with the same pace, halted, slide the cart back and took Fox back to his stall, un-tacked him and gave him his lunch. Fox at this point is only walking twenty minutes at the end of the lesson, so there isn't worry about feeding him.

This was an enlightened opportunity to have Steve observe and comment. He gave several important comments:

1. Careful not to shift the pad under the surcingle when putting on the crupper and push the hair on his back the wrong way.

Important for me because since there isn't a crupper on any of the normal equipment I use, this was a good reminder, and something I didn't think about while using dressage saddles, which are put on and slid back in the direction of the hair.

2. Since we want the tracer to be free to slide back its important the metal ring on the tracer is behind the leather loop rather in front where is might hang up and not be able to be released.

3. The driving harness has a headstall that has binders. Steve wondered if Fox would get any benefit from them. After watching Fox he noticed that Fox is extremely comfortable seeing and feeling the tracers and accepted them as nonthreatening. Fox is also accustomed to the arena so for this level of cart training it's the place that is usual for Fox so it's fine to let him see what he is familiar seeing. If he were to go to other strange places the blinders would perhaps be helpful in limiting his focus.

Monday

- Completed the warm-up longe lesson of walk, trot, and canter.
- I'm assisting because the assistant still has trouble balancing the longe line and driving aid of the whip.
- Interesting happening was while we were longeing, a bird flew into one of the opened bays of one side of the arena. The bird startled Fox as he came around on the circle and he turned away continuing in the other direction. He continued trotting around like nothing had happened. We halted him and merely started him again on the left side. It's not that random happenings occur but how they are handled that makes the difference. It's important to try to minimize distractions at the beginning but birds do fly about.
- The assistant performed the walk on and halts exercise
- Fox was halted and I brought the carriage and slipped the tracers into the leather loops on either side of the surcingle. This time I

took the position to lead Fox and the assistant walked near the cart as the safety position. Fox walked easily without hesitation.

- We now made several turns across the arena and changed direction. He seems totally comfortable. We had him halt and returned him to his stall for lunch.

Tuesday

1. Performed the walk, trot, and canter warm-up
2. Assistant performed the exercise walk on and halt commands
3. Brought Fox to the long side of the arena and slipped the tracers through the leather loops on the surcingle without attaching them
4. Walked around the arena changing directions and practicing halting

- In preparation for actually attaching the driving reins and working while standing back from Fox's shoulder and giving commands I ask Fox to halt and using a short whip I test to make sure that Fox remembers the use of the whip near and behind him. When ridden Fox learned the cross over of the dressage whip over his shoulder to place the rider aid on the inside of the horse when riding in the arena.
- There are two ways this is accomplished: whip raised above the horse and lowered to the opposite side; or flipped by the end reversing it. Booth techniques must be done with care because if the horse catches sight of this object behind his head, it could frighten him.
- After making sure that Fox remembered the whip being used behind him, I now took a position to work from the in-hand position to give the commands. Fox now has the directions coming from his rear quarter instead of his shoulder.

5. He immediately walked when given the walk on command. Fox was halted and with the assistant watchfully with her hand

near the tracers I proceeded to walk around the cart checking on harness as I would have to do making any adjustments. Fox stood at attention as he's been taught. This skill is extremely necessary for a carriage horse and Fox got an A+. We promptly took him back to his stall for lunch.

Wednesday-Fox has a day at Pasture

Thursday

Today's lesson consisted of the sequential lesson plans of previous day's work

1. Performed the walk, trot, and canter warm-up
2. Assistant performed the exercise walk on and halt commands
3. Brought Fox to the long side of the arena and slipped the tracers through the leather loops on the surcingle without attaching them
4. Walked around the arena with the cart changing directions and practicing halting

- The lesson went very smoothly and Fox briskly walked with the cart following the command of 'walk on' and 'halt'.
- Today at the end of the lesson the cart was pulled back and Fox was asked to halt and then take several steps back. The assistant now stood away from Fox and he was standing without any restraint.
- I walked around the cart. Fox watched me but didn't move. Gave the command to stand and continued to walk around and Fox stood perfectly still. I now brought the cart up again and slipped into the leather on the surcingle. Fox continued to stand. I waited a short time and rewarded Fox with a carrot and the stand-in pat/snap of the fingers. Fox is especially alert to the

snap sound. As discussed in the previous chapters it's important to tailor rewards and trained stand—in reward.

- I now have the beginning of working with Fox alone, but I still want the safety factors of the second knowledgeable person, and the cart is still only slipped through the leather and not buckled to the surcingle. Fox is demonstrating good potential for being a good cart candidate.

- Analyzing his progress the outstanding behavior is his ability to stand on command. This command to stand, which he learned as a youngster, is paying off in a positive result because he is so easy to handle with all the potential distractions that go with driving work and harnessing.

- Whenever trainers are involved with a teaching situation, the observant teacher also learns. The stand cue has amazing results, in that it makes the training session positive and easy for the trainer.

Friday

It's important to consistently keep lessons repetitive—repeating the easier learned skills. This is one of the useful techniques of rote learning. Where it's not effective is where the horse/person learning fails to achieve the desired skills. It is here the applied behavior analysis causes the trainer/teacher to stop and reevaluate the lessons.

Even though it may appear that the horse already knows those skills, this provides a basis for teaching the lesson plan. In the event that the horse fails to perform a new skill it is easier to step back to an easier learned skill so that a lessons always ends on correctly performed skills. Review the chapter on "Perfect Practice".

1. Performed the walk, trot, and canter warm-up
2. Assistant performed the exercise walk on and halt commands
3. Brought Fox to the long side of the arena and slipped the tracers through the leather loops on the surcingle without attaching them

4. Walked around the arena with the cart changing directions and practicing halting

Fox performs the basic part of the lesson. For the final part of the lesson reins are attached to the bridle through the surcingle to the correct driving position. I move my position and now stand besides Fox holding the reins. The command to walk is given and Fox walks straight now being commanded with the reins and voice/whip commands. Fox has now successfully combined several important skills.

1. Understands the commands, 'walk on' and 'halt' from the easy position of leading
2. Demonstrates correct longe work walk, trot, and canter
3. **Important**: Confident with the trainer standing close and using the whip as a cue walking around the arena with the reins through the driving surcingle
4. Totally accepts the cart being brought up and walks with the cart in position being driven by with the reins through the surcingle. The trainer walks safely near the rear of Fox, and easily proceeds around the arena using the commands halt and walk on.

Saturday-Pasture day

Sunday

Worked Fox alone— tacked with the surcingle and long reining him from the position of his hindquarters without the cart. The reins are 7- feet long which makes it easier than having the full long reins of 24 feet in my hands. Practice long rein commands, with a change of rein crossing the reins over his back. Fox easily performs the command of walk on and halt. Because of all the work performed with Fox teaching him as a youngster with classical long reins, in preparation for riding, he performs perfectly. Since I am working without the safety of the second person today I don't work with the cart, but I do as a final task is to ask him to stand, bring the cart up into position, and then move it back. Fox shows no concern about the cart being moved behind. Fox stands on the cue he has learned so well and the importance of establishing cues strengthened on primary rewards. It is a successful lesson.

Monday

The lesson with the assistant continues to repeat the lessons skills:

1. Performed the walk, trot, and canter warm-up on the longe line
2. Assistant performed the exercise walk on and halt commands – this continues Fox recognition of the assistant
3. Walked Fox using the reins through the surcingle standing at the hindquarters without the cart command Fox to walk from the new position
4. Brought Fox to the long side of the arena and slipped the cart tracers through the leather loops on the surcingle without attaching them
5. Walked Fox around the arena leading him with the cart changing directions and practicing halting
6. New skills: Command Fox with reins through the surcingle standing at his hindquarters and drive with the cart
7. Assistant walks near able to assist if Fox is confused

NEW skill: Fox now takes cues with the trainer standing from the hindquarter without any reluctance with the trainer using the new position or apprehension of the cue of the whip from the rear position, which could be unsettling for the horse. This is the importance of teaching cue understanding rather than using cues connected with force. If the trainer is throwing ropes, chasing, or waving threatening arms this isn't a horse that understands cues and trusts the trainer to be predictable. Horses that haven't been taught understandable cues could be threatened and try to protect themselves.

Successful Four Weeks

Today is the successful completion of a sequential step-by-step month's lessons of training Fox to become to accept a training cart. There are several main points:

- The assistant for this project was available each day for the training program with Fox. Even though she wasn't experienced with the specifics of longe work, working in hand, or driving, she was an enthusiastic participant and while teaching her she made a valuable connection positive connection to Fox via carrot rewards for standing and stand-in pats.
- The assistant was trained to handle Fox for each training step to ensure that she could step into my place at anytime. This is a safety issue to safeguard the horse and handlers if Fox were to become afraid we would have the extra hands to remove the items; especially when we began working with the cart. This is potentially an extremely dangerous situation having not only the driving reins but the cart as well.
- The training cart because it's so light rests on the leather loop of the surcingle without being buckled to the tracers. This provides a safety factor to easily slide the cart back.
- Having now completed the successful month without mishap and the set-up of using this extremely light training cart is

satisfactory compared to other methods of tying various items to the horse to pull/drag. Pulling wasn't the beginning primary concern, but rather accustoming Fox to the tracers at his side and something 'strange' following him. Since part of the difficulty and safety of working with horses is the potential quick response to being frightened, this was a primary concern that Fox was systematically and slowly introduced to each step— no thirty minute instant carriage horse!

- Each lesson was based on the previous lessons, which were reviewed with a two-day lesson repeat before adding the new skills. As with all effective educational programs, every part of reaching the goal of having Fox to accept being commanded from the cart was broken down into small learnable steps.

The Learnable Steps

1. Understands the commands, 'walk on' and 'halt' in the easy position of leading
2. Demonstrates correct longe work walk trot and canter
3. Confident with the trainer standing close and using the whip as a cue walking around the arena with the reins through the driving surcingle
d. Totally accepts the cart being brought up and walks with the cart in position being driven by with the reins through the surcingle. The trainer walks safely near the rear of Fox, and easily proceeds around the arena with the commands: halt and walk on.

- **NEW** At the end of the lesson the assistant stands with Fox, giving him the stand command. I enter the cart sit for several minutes, the assistant rewards Fox, and I exit. Fox is unharnessed and taken to his stall for lunch. We are totally happy about the success and how easily Fox has learned these lessons. Positive work yields positive horses.

Tuesday

Today's lesson is a repeat of Monday with the focus of repetition. At this stage Fox has the important skills necessary to work with the training cart.

1. The longe work at the beginning is to ensure that Fox stays physically fit to perform the basic riding cues of walk, trot, and canter.
2. Work in hand with the shorter driving rides is to practice the skill given by the trainer working safely near Fox directing him to walk and halt on commands.
3. The cart is easily put in place with the tracers slipped through the surcingle loop to ensure the safety of releasing the cart if necessary.
4. Fox is walked around the arena with the trainer directing him with the reins simulating the commands that will be given when the trainer is seated in the cart.
5. Halt Fox and enter the cart and Fox stands quietly.
6. Since the lessons skills are accomplished Fox goes back to his stall for lunch

Wednesday / Thursday Fox has two well-deserved pasture days

Friday Take photos

1. Complete longe exercise
2. Walk/Halt with longe reins practicing commands
3. Attached cart and practice command with the trainers walking next to Fox
4. End lesson sitting in cart- Fox stands perfectly at the halt.

Saturday First Ride in the Cart

Reviewed all exercises

1. Complete longe exercise.
2. Walk/Halt with longe reins practicing commands.
3. Attached cart and practice command with the trainers walking next to Fox.
4. Fox stands perfectly at the halt I enter the cart and sit quietly.
5. The command to walk on is given and Fox walks with the cart gliding easily behind Fox- the cart still isn't buckled to the tracer in case we had to release the cart. Fox is totally directed from the cart with the longer reins.
6. The positive part of using the training cart is how light and easily it moves behind the horse.

Sunday

- Reviewed all exercises: Longe exercise, walk/halt commands, and attaching cart walking along directing Fox from his side.
- The cart is still attached by only resting the tracer on the surcingle leather loop. The lightness of the cart and the cart occupant make this possible and include a element of safety. The chest harness, which would allow Fox to pull heavier weights

over ground, isn't attached because we're working in a perfectly groomed arena.

- The focus of the lesson is now to give Fox time walking around the arena making rein changes. This is now an important phase to allow Fox to practice his new skill in the controlled environment of the arena.

Monday

- Reviewed longe work walk, trot, and canter. This beginning work is performed for two reasons: review of commands and exercise.
- Since the driving work doesn't consist of much strenuous work the longe work is important to keep Fox fit since he isn't being ridden for his normal forty-five minutes since the focus is on the driving skills.
- Today we work on long reins commands with the trainer walking at Fox's hindquarter. Fox is very comfortable with this close position of the trainer because of previous extensive work. It's important to practice rein commands before driving from the cart. This review is to ensure that Fox remembers the rein commands. Ask Fox to back into the tracers of the cart, which will make it easier to hook Fox to the cart single-handed.

Tuesday-Wednesday- Thursday

Fox gets a few days off from the routine with nice weather he gets to go out to his pasture.

Friday

- Working alone today's review is the longe lessons of walk, trot, and canter. This work is to constantly review commands and to also provide fifteen minutes of exercise that isn't part of the long rein and cart work.

- Spend about 10-minutes to review long rein work with changes of rein to make sure that Fox understands the commands coming from behind him via the whip and sounds.
- Ask Fox to halt. The driving reins are attached. Walk Fox near the cart, ask him to halt and attach the cart through the surcingle leathers without securing the tracers.
- Standing near the cart, the command to walk on is given. Fox obediently walks around the arena. Fox is asked to halt and I enter the cart. Fox is given the command to walk on and continues around the arena.
- The direction to cross the arena is given. Fox hesitates; I give the command to walk on he takes another step but again stops. I understand that Fox is uncertain because he very so slightly moves backwards. I stay extremely quiet with the driving aid, so not to frighten him. I quietly ask him to walk on and Fox begins to walk to the other side of the arena. This is a new sensation because Fox, even though the cart is light, is now pulling it with the surcingle. The breast harness isn't attached because to move the light training cart on the arena surface isn't needed. At this beginning stage it's important for Fox to practice the simple skill of walking around the arena with the cart. It's important to verify that Fox is totally confident with this new skill before securely attaching the cart.
- The plan at this stage is to allow Fox successful practice to have him gain positive driving skills before adding new tasks.

Saturday

- Pouring loud rain on the arena roof with rain blowing in open bay
- Performed the longe lesson for the fifteen-minute exercise at walk, trot, and canter.

- Fox is a little more apprehensive as he is more focused on the loud sound of the rain. While performing as expected, Fox is not totally focused on me even though he hasn't made errors. The long rein lesson walking around the arena making rein changes is continued. Fox doesn't walk close to the long wall that has the open bays because a small amount of rain is blowing into arena. Fox behaves obediently to the long rein commands, which are given walking at his hind quarters.

- Give Fox the command to halt and walk around him adjusting various parts of the harness to test his ability to stand. I bring the cart up but don't attach it. Fox continues to stand. Decide to end the lesson at this successful point, because I can see the weather is getting louder and potentially more distracting. Fox continues to stand while the long reins are undone.

- We end on a successful note- very important—perfect practice. Fox goes back to his stall for a small afternoon snack.

- There is often a tendency to extend a lesson. If perfect practice is considered, and the fact that horses stick to learned behavior, it's better to stop earlier on a positive performance. There is strong research to support emphasizing quality rather than quantity.

Sunday

- Decide to assess where Fox is in the training. Outfit him with the surcingle without the crupper. Start the lesson by attaching driving reins and asking Fox to stand. While holding the reins, I pick up the tracers to the cart and bring the cart up to Fox. Fox stands perfectly still.

- He waits until I give the walk on command and from outside the cart drive Fox around the arena making rein changes across the centerline. Fox is asked to halt and I enter the cart. After waiting, the command walk on is given. He begins to walk around the arena and is asked for several halts.

- It's a positive note to end the lesson. Fox patiently stands while all the reins and tack are removed. This is a large part of the driving work, because of many more harness pieces connected with driving. This is where the characteristic of the horse to dependably stand is extremely important. Besides the horse temperament, systematic training to stand on cue is important. Training on cues adds the dimension of repetitive skills rather than randomly depending on a good-natured horse.

Monday

- Planned to work Fox but things became disorganized with the assistant's change of schedule – ended up scrapping the training plan.
- Had Fox all tacked with a new clean white pad to take some pictures.
- Fox was standing perfectly when I was distracted and forgot where I placed the reins while turning my attention behind me.
- Fox always stands perfectly and I can walk around him, but today my behavior is different because of the change in schedule. He assumes with this change he is free as he is often allowed to be free in the arena after work.
- So Fox decided to walk away to the middle of the arena and lie down and roll on his nice clean pad! Horses pick up on distractions and change of routine. I've learned this is the time to stop because of my disorganization. No harm done except to the clean while pad. I give Fox the 'come' signal and he came and promptly stood in front of me—as he always does after his free time.
- Risk management guidelines support that many accidents happen with changes in routine and unfocused behavior.
- Using a safe training environment such as a fenced area is important. To assume a horse with all types of attached lines

and harness won't possibly get free isn't proactive. Perfect practice precludes most risk but not all.

Tuesday

- Good lesson with Fox
- Spent twenty minutes walk, trot, and canter. Making the longe lesson more energetic so there is a part of exercise for Fox since the carriage work is done at the walk. After the longe lesson, the long driving reins are connected and a practice session with commands to walk and halt are practiced. Since the directions come from a distance rather than the rider position it's important to make certain that the horse understand the commands given through the voice and driving whip.
- The cart is attached. Fox stands perfectly at liberty while the trainer walks around moving the cart in place. The command to walk on is given and Fox obediently walks around the arena. Fox is asked to halt and the trainer enters the cart. Fox is commanded to walk on. He walks and then halts— seeming unsure. To make sure that Fox is not confused and perhaps upset, I get out of the cart and drive him from the ground. He immediately moves forward. It would be an error to overuse the whip with Fox since he is normally obedient to cues from the whip. It would also be an error to assume that Fox understands all the driving commands at this stage, because he has been a pleasant horse to train.
- Continued walking around the arena driving from the ground, halting. End the lesson with a final halt. Fox stands perfectly. This is an example of how important the stand 'cue' becomes. It's really important not to have force or stress connected with the halt.

Wednesday - Day off

Thursday

1. Fox performed an energetic longe lesson. He is sometimes slow to get moving until he performs canter work. With some horses, canter work is an effective method for impulsion rather than harsher aids.
2. He listens to commands to walk, trot, and canter, and halt. He especially stands on the halt command, which makes it very easy to assemble the cart harnessing.
3. Reviewed commands given from the rear position, because I notice the previous lesson in the cart that Fox seemed uncertain about the commands when given from the cart. It was decided I would practice commands from the ground walking by the cart in preparation for the next session sitting in the cart.

Friday

*   Longe lesson pressing Fox for an energetic trot and canter. Extremely windy day with outside noise so today's lesson is focused on the commands to walk and halt.
*   He needs work and sometimes need refocus on the cue to walk. Since he isn't wearing blinders I notice he slightly glances behind when the voice and whip command is given as if he isn't sure but has to look to see what he has to do. Fox is cooperative and only needs review.

Saturday and Sunday Day off

Monday

*   Fox performs a longe lesson with surcingle in preparation for the driving lessons. Exercise walk, trot, and canter.

- Fox is at the point of maintenance so it's important to repetitively practice the new skill of driving with the cart. The cart still hasn't been attached by buckling the leather tugs on the surcingle and the chest attachment to the actual cart. I want to assure that the skill of pulling the cart and following commands is well learned.
- Fox stands perfectly while I slip the tracers in the leather tugs without buckling them in place. We walk around the arena with me driving from the ground and in the cart.
- Fox is doing increasing more consistent work from inside the cart.

Wednesday- Thursday Day off

Friday

Fox is on a skill maintenance program to practice so all previous skills are practiced

1. Longe lesson
2. Fox stands perfectly still while I attach reins and cart
3. Walk around the arena making rein changes across the middle
4. I enter the cart for a short stretch around the arena, halt and exit
5. Fox is halted and the cart taken back
6. Back to stall and untacked
7. Fox has become very consistent and the process very successful so far

Monday

- Today's lesson went as normal until the last segment with the cart. The lesson was proceeding as normal with Fox waking around the arena with the cart when a loud noise outside upset Fox and he suddenly moved to the right to see what happened.
- Of course because Fox was attached to the cart and the straight tracers, he couldn't easily turn and started to shift the cart sideways

with his motion. This is the perfect reason that no matter how well the lessons proceeds the trainer should never assume a quick lesson is sufficient. I immediately, while standing at the left to fox, asked him to halt and he came to a halt. This is an example that a lesson plan should include many repetitions. Fox could have become very upset because he couldn't turn as he is accustomed to while ridden. He was immediately calm because of his positive connection with the all the positive lessons and my presence. The positive presence of the trainer is greatly underestimated—the trainer becomes a positive stand-in reinforcer.

- Having a horse attached to a cart or carriage is a formidable task and not to be take lightly. A rider in a saddle has the possibility to dismount, but in the event of an attached cart there is a more serious potential of an entanglement.

- Fox has learned the stand/halt command so well that even under duress he responds and I can honestly say I am always pleasantly surprised how well this learned command works.

- We proceeded successfully with the rest of the lesson.

Fox celebrates successful cart training!

Summary

Fox has continued with the lessons for several weeks more with the tracers not permanently attached to the cart. Shortly, in the next months thereafter the lessons were ended with attaching the cart with all the attachments connected to the cart. He has continued with no difficulties to have the other pieces of the cart attached.

Key Points

- Basic cue to stand is extremely important for several aspects of working with horses.
- Whether on the ground or in the saddle having a horse stand on cue- without force- is imperative for ensuring safe work with our companions.
- It's important not to threaten or punish horses to get them to stand.
- The reliability of a forced cue is undependable compared to a positively learn cue. This is an example of something learned in a pleasant environment.
- The lessons of teaching a horse to pull a cart were safely accomplished by following a sequence of skills.
- Risk Management: All tasks with horses should have some risk assessment for safe procedures.
- Providing extensive practice is important to have the reliability of safe performance.

Firestar and the 'Yahoo'

The following occurrence is an example of how quickly an aggressive act, no matter how insignificant the action may appear to the horse handler, may begin negative horse behavior. Several horse training methods unnecessarily invite a physical negative response from the horse. Naturally horses have few methods for self-protection against what may appear as a threatening action. Most methods of horse training rely on some systematic method of acclimatizing the animals to humans and the environments to reduce the element of surprise. Systematically most horse training methods use repetitive signals that the horse understands.

Surprise is an element that hinders animal training because of the unknown element of a sudden occurrence.

The above picture is when Firestar a large seventeen hands warmblood born on the farm; systematically trained and a fine easy-going stallion, he easily began his training under saddle. He has never demonstrated any aggression toward trainers and farm personnel. Even as a young colt, he was never handled roughly but rather easily learned to stand on cue when 3-months-old. When we needed to have his attention, he was given the stand cue. A horse cannot engage in the behavior of nipping and standing quietly at the same time. Because Firestar learned the stand cue so easily, he was never yelled at or negatively physically handled.

Firestar, now twelve years old, was gelded to allow him more freedom. The late change from stallion to gelding didn't alter his personality; he was still the same sensitive, easy to handle and ride horse. All of our stall cleaners, veterinarian, and farrier loved him and marveled how well-behaved he was. This made the following happening very unbelievable.

I have always made it a practice to follow new stall cleaners the first few days when they are in the stalls with the horses. The horses are free in fifteen by twenty feet stalls and are trained to be feed in a corner and not to interact during this time. New stall cleaners who also worked at other barns are always amazed how the horses all go to their corner and never make any attempt to bother them, much less the horrific stories I've been told about some of their experiences.

A new stall cleaner was hired and I accompanied her the first 3 days so she wouldn't be worried about the horses being free in the stall. The newest worker was amazed as all her predecessors were about how the horses quietly stayed in their spot eating their meal.

Everything went perfectly with the new worker, until one day I happened to look out while she rode the ATV heading to clean the first stall. On the back of the ATV she had a passenger who was wildly gesticulating with his arms while they rode to the front barn.

My risk management alert told me I needed to check this out. I didn't need an impractical teenager yelling in the horse stall. I ran through the back of the barn and arrived to look at the back of Firstar's stall to hear the wild teenager yell "get over there". My nice quiet stall cleaner was telling him to get away from the horse and be quiet. In the next moment I was now looking over the stall wall and with my best teacher voice loudly said, "Get out of the stall." He now hastily retreated to his pickup truck and I walked around to the front door to Firstar's stall. Firestar was standing in his spot eating, but I could see he wasn't his normal self. He was furtively looking at us as if he thought something was going to happen.

Apparently what had happened was that when my nice quiet stall cleaner walked in the stall, her young friend who thought that he should show his horse dominating technique decided to tell Firestar where he should stand, by smacking his rump and yelling at him. I often clean stalls on staff days off so I know everyone of my horses. I've knocked them with the rake, bumped into them while walking around the stall, and even occasionally my Great Dane walks in the stall to see what's going on. I've even occasionally wanted them to move if they were stepping on dirty bedding. They're so accustomed to this procedure they all gently pick up the hoof and keep eating.

Firestar was now nervous when approached toward his rear and made a half-hearted motion with his hind leg as if he needed to warn and protect himself against the person in his stall; including me! I had trained him since his birth on the farm, so it was my responsibility to solve this now beginning negative behavior; before it became serious.

This is an example of how quickly bad horse behavior may randomly be learned. The next part of this chapter is the explanation and how Firestar was retrained and his trust restored.

Reestablish Cues

- When Firstar was a 3-months-old colt he was taught the cue to stand.
- The next steps were to easily approach and touch him using the cue to stand.

- This behavior was developed to stand and be able to easily slip a halter on (outlined in *Behavior Modification for Horses with pictures of the cute Firestar and his mom*).
- The next behavior was picking up his feet.

Plan to Stop Negative Behavior

The plan was to use the positive behavior that Firestar already knew standing on cue and picking up his feet on cue. Incompatible behavior is a technique that uses one behavior that can't be performed at the same time as the negative behavior.

Firestar couldn't be picking up his feet on cue and menacing the handler at the same time. This is an example of incompatible behavior. Several days were spent not only cleaning his stall but also going in his stall several times and picking up his feet. On the first day Firestar showed mild distress when approached on the left rear quarter. Interestingly he showed no negative behavior on the right side either walking to his front or rear quarter.

Day 1

Since I knew and trained Firestar from birth, I did the training. While cleaning the stall the new helper cleaned on the far side of his 15 by 20 large stall. I walked and cleaned around Firestar during this time and asked him to pick up his feet. I tried to create the occurrence of what had initially frightened him. We identified that I wasn't so much the negative cue, but the new stall cleaner. Even though she had nothing to do with the previous event in his stall, the horse identified the new person as potentially threatening.

Day 2

I accompanied the new stall cleaner so we could monitor Firestar's reaction. We noticed he was nervous as he began the ritual of standing on the side of the stall and eating. He again initially moved his left hoof slightly as he noticed the new person enter his stall, as if expecting the need to protect himself. After we entered the stall and began the routine he returned to eating and seemed relaxed. Again the new cleaner stayed cleaning on the far side of the stall and I asked Firestar to pick up his feet while walking round close to him and cleaning with the rake. Again I returned to the stall latter and asked him to perform his normal tasks of standing on cue, putting on the saddle, and bridling. He behaved as always.

Day 3

Again I accompanied the new stall cleaner into the stall and she filled his feed dish. Firestar seemed to notice the new cleaner but performed his usual ritual of standing in the accustomed place and eating. The plan was to have the new stall cleaner do the far side of the stall while I worked closely around Firestar. Occasionally I asked him for his feet, randomly rewarding him, while brushing the rake against his leg…he immediately picked his foot up thinking I wanted to clean under his hoof as usual. I even brushed up against his rump.

Day 4

Obviously Firestar knows me very well and in all his training never received yelling, smacking, or roping. From the time he was less than 3-months-old he was taught the cue to stand at liberty—with no chasing. Now it was time to see how he felt about the new person. During the cleaning we now quietly changed positions. Firestar kept eating and paid no attention. My new stall cleaner and I stood side by side on his left side near his front leg. I told her to ask him for his hoof. Firestar immediately presented his hoof.

Day 5

I accompanied the new stall cleaner but only stayed by the door. Firestar seemed his normal self and everything went as planned. At the end of the cleaning session she asked for Firstar's hoof.

The success of turning around the start of the beginning of what could become dangerous behavior now restored Firstar to his previous behavior. When my normal farrier came to do hoofs, I alerted him even though he has known Firstar for many years since Firstar was a young colt. The old Firestar was back and in part due to the skills previously taught and now retrieved.

Key Points

- Horses easily connect a single frightening experience to people or cues.
- If there is a basic positive level of training, it's easier to return to that positive behavior.
- It's important to identify the now negative cue and behavior and reverse the result.
- Using the technique of incompatible behavior, a horse cannot cooperatively offer the hoof and threaten with that hoof at the same time.
- As offering the cooperative hoof is **increased**, any threatening behavior is **decreased**.
- It was fortunate that Firstar never escalated to more than an understated motioning with his leg.
- It was very important to reverse this beginning behavior before it became serious.
- Any aggressive action upon our part would have escalated Firstar's fear. Unfortunately, there is little information about the technique incompatible behavior and force is unscientifically applied.

Jewel: A Case Study-Reversing

Chasing a Horse With Plastic

Jewel is an eleven-year-old Hungarian mare that is being evaluated for training. She has previously been handled and not afraid of people. However, she had a rough transport experience because a blue plastic tarp was used to scare her into the horse trailer for transport. The crude techniques of using plastic bags to frighten a horse to move somewhere rather than teaching a taught cue is common with some horse training groups. First we're told to use plastic bags to frighten the horse to make them move forward and then to repeatedly hit them with plastic bags so they're not afraid of plastic bags. This is a self-defeating method.

The owner would like to see how behavior modification techniques would help her to become a pleasurable mount and less unsafe on the ground. Today's lesson was to evaluate Jewel and see if she was receptive to learning cues for ground obedience that will be used to get a rider into the saddle. The owner already established her interest in carrots. An animal's interest in food reward increases the reliability of learning a cue and also to only needing a few repetitions compared to working over several days. The owner had hung the infamous blue tarp on the railing of the indoor arena, where Jewel resided to become accustomed to her new surroundings. The arena is a safe environment to work with the horse, with a secure wall.

We walked up to Jewel and offered her a carrot that she happily ate.

The sound of a snap of fingers (snap of fingers can be used as a stand-in signal to connect the food reward or any other signals) is paired to offering the carrot. The cue was repeated each time Jewel walked to me. I didn't have to wait until Jewel decided she would come, but used the command 'come'. No one had to chase her around. She also came to me while I stood near the blue tarp and while she looked apprehensive, she came and stood next to me. After repeating the cue and getting Jewel to come on the cue 'come' we could go to anyplace in the small arena and ask Jewel to 'come' and she would immediately walk to the owner and stand waiting for the reward. Besides the command 'come' our presence became the positive stand-in cue. The simple explanation for this method is that the horse very quickly recognizes a positive situation: positive cue and positive response.

Table 11 Teaching Horse to Come on Cue

Cue	Behavior	Reward/Reinforcer
Command given within close range of the horse. * **'Come'**	Horse comes to owner	**Primary reinforcers** given upon behavior
* When this cue was taught to 3–month-old colt Star, it was taught in his stall. Since Jewel was off-loaded into the small arena, the teaching was done in this environment rather than to precipitously move her because she was calm in the surroundings.		**Secondary reinforcers** given at the same time as the food: obvious signal, pat, noise, etc. At the beginning this signal is done with the food rewards and becomes paired with the food and becomes associated or a stand-in for food.

Since Jewel has been kindly handled by people and the only impasse is the frightening experience of being chased with the 'blue tarp', a light string halter is put on. She is asked several times to 'come' and is rewarded and the string halter taken off.

The successful lesson is repeated several days while Jewel become accustomed to her new home. The lesson is so successful that as soon as the owner approaches Jewel comes and stands in front of her. This is significant because the owner has become a recognizable positive cue in addition to the command 'come'.

Key Points

- Cues are easily taught by pairing the command with a reinforcers- both food and taught stand-in.
- It is important the horses aren't trained using frightening cues to get them to perform.
- Frightening cues, while getting the horse to perform, will often remain in memory and surface at inopportune times.
- Positive horses need to be trained with positive methods.

Lesson 2

We proceeded to the next step. The next step was to teach Jewel to walk forward using the cue 'walk on'. Since she has been handled, she allowed the light halter to be put on. She had been led but is inconsistent the behavior and cues weren't learned. When the owner tried to lead her she would turn in on the handler making a dangerous situation for the trainer. The problem of the horse turning in on the handler is a typical fault. Teaching the correct 'walk on' command solves this difficulty whereby the handler walking at the shoulder of the horse gives the command 'walk on' and the horse walks forward. The horse is not pulled or restrained by the lead line but is taught to walk straight. The correct command to move forward 'walk on' is being taught that will be used for future training in the saddle or other disciplines. When the horse is commanded to move forward, it moves by a taught cue. This cue when taught on the ground will be use to tell the horse to 'walk on' while mounted.

She is unafraid so the dressage whip that is carried in the correct position in the right hand when walking to the left. Whips are taught as non-threatening aids to instruct the horse to move forward–a pointer. She is given the 'walk on' command and gently without pulling her inward and giving the verbal command to step forward. After one or two steps Jewel is told to 'whoa' and stop. She is immediately given the carrot reward. We make several attempts rewarding each correct approximation. As long as she walks on and halts, she is rewarded. The owner uses the word 'whoa' for stop. She is very responsive. When Jewel is unsure of the 'walk on' cue, the hand is used in front of her nose and give her the first command we practiced —come. This relying on the 'come' cue is only to help clarify to Jewel what we want her to perform. This technique is called luring and should be sparingly used. It's also helpful at this beginning stage to have an assistant who can also softly encourage the forward steps. The technique helps the horse to approximate the desired action until performed solely on cue.

The trainer is persistently patient that she halts straight ––looking ahead before the reward is given. The reward is never given for other behavior. At this point even if she stops, she is rewarded seeking to improve each response for accuracy. At the beginning mistakes are accepted, because it demonstrates the horse trying to perform. By the end of twenty minutes she is walking straight on and halting on command, not always halting perfectly straight but stopping on command and improving each attempt.

The owner takes over to repeat the work. The trial starts easily but on the halt she turns in pushing the owner with her shoulder. This is a complaint of many trying to lead horses. The correction is not to be overly strong with the lead line. The horse is allowed to move and halt without undue pressure but relies on teaching cues rather than pressure.

The correct behavior is demonstrated that the light use of the lead line creates the difference. Jewel walks on around the arena edge. The same spot is used to halt and to assist the learning along with immediately rewarding correct behavior.

Rewarding behavior with food is extremely powerful and not to be taken lightly. The horse isn't ignorant. They know that the trainer has food just like I know where I have cookies hidden. The horse will try to get the reward for other behavior. It's the trainer's responsibility to make sure that only the correct behavior is rewarded, with the taught cue, and immediately rewarded ideally within 2-seconds. The owner corrects the response and produces three totally correct walk on and halts. We stop on this very successful session.

Besides the teaching of cues, 'walk on' and 'halt', the horse learns associated behavior with the movement or no movement of the trainer. The subtle cues are additionally important but the voice cues become **extremely** strong, because they were initially taught with the strength of food and also taught with the stand-in cues. These cues become so strong that even when horses are under duress they react to learned cues that are strongly imbedded into their reactions and often override natural behavior.

These methods have years of research to support their use. Granted, laboratory research has the benefit of a controlled environment, but if the trainer takes care about the horse environment to establish the initial cues is as effective.

Table 12 Teaching the Horse the Cue 'Walk on'

Cue	Behavior	Reward/Reinforcer
Command given within close range of the horse. '**Walk on**'	Horse walks forward a few steps- using the wall of the arena	**Primary reinforcers** given upon behavior

		Secondary reinforcers given at the same time as the food: obvious signal, pat, noise, etc. At the beginning this signal is done with the food rewards and becomes paired with the food and becomes associated or a stand-in for food
Command **'Whoa'**	Horse stops on command-	**Primary reinforcers** given upon behavior
		Secondary reinforcers given at the same time as the food: obvious signal, pat, noise, etc.

Key Points

- Cues are systematically taught using primary and secondary reinforcers.
- Cues are carefully practiced until learned before adding other skills.
- Horses become calm and responsive as the same cues are used and strengthen with reinforcers.

Lesson 3

The owner has practiced the skills 'come' when she passes the arena. Jewel now comes when she sees the owner approach and hears the command 'come'. As long as she walks on and halts she is rewarded.

She is very responsive. When Jewel is unsure of the walk on cue, The hand motions in front of her nose to focus and remind her as the first command practiced –come. The trainer is insistent that she halts straight looking ahead before the reward is given. At this point even if she stops, she is rewarded seeking to improve each response. By the end of 20 minutes she is walking straight on and halting on command, not always halting perfectly straight but stopping on command and improving each attempt.

Rewarding behavior with food is extremely powerful and not to be taken lightly. The horse isn't ignorant. You don't need clickers or gadgets, because the horse connects the food reward to sound and visual cues, you don't need a gadget to train cues. They know that the trainer has food, and the horse will try to get the reward for other behavior. It's the trainer's responsibility to make sure that only the correct behavior is rewarded and immediately within 2 seconds ideally. The owner corrects the response and produces three totally correct walk on and halts. We stop on this very successful session. It is important to stop the lesson upon correct behavior.

Key Points

- Risk management: Teaching learned cues assures more safety when working with horses
- It's important to teach stand-in or secondary reinforcers to a cue that you always have with you. Horses are different from other animals worked on the ground.
- Cues to come, stop, and stand are extremely important when an extenuating situation arises- reinforced cues become so strong, horses will come on command and stand in a liberty environment.
- The **Stand** safety cue works and precludes using unnecessary aggressive control.

Lesson

1. Cue: come on cue using snap instantly as horse comes to trainer rewarded with trainer. Work in the area of the blue tarp. Repeat command several times and at this stage of learning reward every time. Later it will move to a random schedule.

2. Put the lovely light halter on- this is a very nice halter for beginning.

3. Cue to stand- I found the arm up with the sound 'Stand' works for me but any other signals will work but should be consistent For me both are important because the verbal cue will be used in the saddle.

4. There is no reason to use 'clicker cues' when a simple voice command works. This was very obvious when I took lessons in Germany and the Reitmaster called "Shritt" to the horses. The word was drawn out and the horses all immediately came to the walk. Since I trained for over thirteen years in Germany and imported the horses I trained, I continue to use Germany commands including the sound to slow down …brrrr …slowly said and the 'r' rolled. Whoa slowly pronounced works also. Clear sound words are very horse effective.

5. Cue 'Walk On' with lead line in hand and whip between trainer and the horse give the command "Walk on" If she freezes bring the hand in front using the 'Snap' and 'come' and reward. This is now being used to help learn the new cue of "Walk on"

6. Cue to 'Halt' Use the same spot in the arena facing away from the view of the outdoors. This is an example of how the environment is used to shape behavior

7. Progressively try to seek the behavior of halting on the 'Voice' and very little use of the longe line. This is where the trainer carefully observes the horse to make small corrections. She is an excellent subject because the whip may be used as a directional wand—like an orchestra conductor.

Key Points

- The effort training horses is an artistic procedure whereby the trainer constantly evaluates behavior and makes a decision about a response. It's always changing whether working with humans or animals.
- Remember you the trainer becomes a secondary reward as the horse associates a positive connection with the trainer.

Session

Jewel has her grass hay served under the blue tarp and immediately comes when the owner approaches. She performs the come and stand cue. Owner says she eventually walks off but this behavior is an excellent start.

Today we put on the light leather longe cavesson so the longe line is correctly used on the nose, which encourages movement forward. As all headgear, the cavesson accurately fitted and adjusted to ensure no interference of the eye or nose. When the halter is used with the longe attached under the nose it actually pulls the horse away toward the trainer not allowing the correct forward motion. We undo all the buckles to attach the cavesson, which is heavier than the halter in little increments to make the process less invasive. Jewel demonstrates total confidence and no apprehension from the handlers.

Jewel was often easily worried, (horses often exhibit worried behavior when they don't understand commands), but she is more confident since she has securely learned skills. She was difficult to safely manage on the ground as she would begin to move erratically making it difficult for the person handling her. Her behavior is not directed toward the handler but rather random and undirected movements because of lacking training and learned cues. So far, she has learned these four commands:

1 Come
2 Stand

3   Walk on

4   Halt

She eventually will be safer for the handler, but these commands will have to be practiced before they override the moments of distraction.

With the cavesson and longe line, Jewel is given the command to 'walk on'. The handler holds the line in the left hand with the dressage whip length in the right to teach the correct cues go forward and halt. These cues are important because they will eventually be used for riding. These are the correct positions of working in hand as described by Heinrich's book (2001) and correct longe work. In his book *Schooling Horses in Hand,* he details, the classical art of longeing. The importance in the beginning stages of training the horse quietly learns the necessary basic skills needed for any safe rideable horse.

Walk around the arena on the left rein—meaning the handler is walking by the shoulder on the left.

Ask Jewel to halt in the same area. She immediately halts on the sound cue.

a.   She is rewarded immediately and doesn't look for the reward. If she were to move toward me, I would place the whip between us to define the command.

b.   Wait for the correct response and reward.

The lesson went so well the trainer was able to step back and give the command from the longe line position. It now didn't make any difference if I stood walking near her shoulder or I stepped back about 10 feet. This is excellent progress, because she has learned the correct command and demonstrated that she understands the commands.

Jewel occasionally makes a 'correct' mistake meaning that she halts or walks on without the command. These mistakes aren't corrected at the beginning of learning a new lesson, because it's the horse trying to do what the trainer is asking for. The correction is merely to ask again and reward. We changed to the other side to walk to the right. This is the reason that trainers train both sides of the horse. Jewel had difficulty performing the behavior equally with the trainer now walking on the right shoulder without an assistant following behind.

Since the right rein command isn't as effective, it's suggested that second person working as an assistant can reinforce the correct behavior on the right. It's important that horses practice as much correct behavior in the learning stage. The practice on the right rein should be practiced with Jewel being asked to come to the trainer moving in that direction. She is not comfortable seeing the trainer by the right shoulder. This was performed several times correctly, rewarded, and discontinued the lesson. It isn't prudent to persist, but rather than persisting, we move back to the level that Jewel can perform, and stop the lesson on a positive performance.

Key Points

- Horses with little experience become safe to handle by teaching cues.
- Four cues: Come, walk-on, halt, and stand are taught to make horses safe to handle.
- Cues aren't only specific to ground behavior but are easily transfer into the saddle or teaching a horse to drive with a carriage. The sound to move forward will be used on the ground and from the saddle.
- The command to stand becomes useful when mounting, asking horses to stand quietly while riding.
- All cues follow an educational approach to teaching a sequence of skills, not only a cutesy trick on the ground.
- The skill sequence is:
  1. safe work on the ground
  2. skills for correct longe work
  3. cues that will also be used for riding work

Summary

Jewel was happily able to walk safely to her pasture, to the relief of her owner who was rightly concern about leading jewel. The owner, similar to other horse owners, believes if you give horses treats they will bite. She was amazed how quickly the lessons were learned. In fact, she learned the 'come' within a few tries. The next day as soon as the horse saw the owner, she came to the arena barrier.

After the week, Jewel while free in her pasture would come on cue—a clear reduction in stress doing normal activities. This owner had trained many youngsters to compete in winning halter classes. Her normal rote training methods using clear commands and calm repetitions were clearly effective. She saw clearly how powerful initially using primary reinforcers are when teaching beginning cues. After the cues are taught the next phase using the secondary reinforcer or stand in becomes effective in continuing positive feedback for the horse. The totally goal surrounding the learning environment becomes positive-creating **Positive Horses.**

Story of Great Dane Allie Teaching a Safety Cue

This is the story of a black Great Dane and the importance of teaching cues not only for performance but also for safety. This story is not only important because it demonstrates the teaching of a cue but also the strong connection that is created when we teach in a positive environment. It began when then three-month old Alexandria, Allie for short, arrived on the farm. We had tried unsuccessfully to rescue a Great Dane and to the chagrin of my two vets who have known us for over fifteen years, including six other Great Danes, we were turned down because we had horses.

Anyone who has had experience with Great Danes and horses know that they aren't herding dogs and are not inclined to chase, and get along with horses. So a picture of the cutest black Great Dane puppy for sale jumped up on the Internet with a reputable breeder. She was the exactly like one of the first black Great Danes I had owned in Spain; so it was love at first sight.

Allie arrived on the farm and began to explore her new home, which included a horse safe fence around a 4-acre part of the farm surrounding the house. For the first several months we oversaw her outdoor excursions. Allie didn't want to be out of our sight, which was good. She never had to be put in her travel container and rarely was on a leash. As Allie gained physical strength, we took her for walks on the back of the farm, which consisted of open fields and a manmade canal that had been used to irrigate the farm when it was a dairy. Just as a young horse is conditioned slowly as to not stress bones and muscles, we progressively increased the length of the outings. She now was eighty pounds and pronounced very fit by her vet. We now had to keep up with her as she ran through the huge field. We came up with the idea of teaching her to go along with the farm ATV, so we could keep an eye on her. At first we started very slowly with mostly walk and increasing a short stretch of running, Pretty soon she was running ahead of us circling around and coming back, taking huge leaps in the air to see where we were.

Concerned about Allie's safety as she took little outings to check interesting smells while she waited for us to catch up, it became important to teach her the safety cue that we teach all the horses on the farm: Come. Allie as all the horses was taught to come on a command and was rewarded with a treat. We wanted to make sure that anytime we called the cue 'Allie-Allie' she would immediately come and we could make sure she was safe. We practiced the cue to make sure she would come even when distracted.

The canal that runs the length of the backfield was potentially unsafe for a young dog that might unwittingly fall into the canal, which was somewhat hidden by tall grass. We wanted to make sure that she would come. A soft rope was also carried in the ATV just in the event that her curiosity to explore might result in a slip into the canal. The problem with this manmade canal is not because it is that deep but that it has the steep sides that would make it difficult to climb out.

The story continues to this past January. Allie is now 2 and a half years old, weighs 180 pounds of solid muscle and can easily run 25 miles an hours. She can overtake the ATV going twenty mph, taking giant leaps through the fields having great sport. Since some of the backfields now contain what is called areas of wetlands they can have about 8-10 inches of water. Allie now has decided this is wonderful playground and great fun to bound over the sections of fields that now in winter are wet. We follow her watching from the dry sections of the field. Her stride is so long that it looks as if she is running on top of the wetland.

Allie and I are finishing our run and have stopped along the canal to enjoy the scenery on the other side. It has turned dark and the moon is beautifully reflected on the wetland field. We are heading back on the dry side of the canal. Allie is sitting right next to me when I see she is intently staring across to the canal to the far trees next to the shining wetland field. She sees something and I strain to see what Allie is staring at in the far distance when an ominous dark cloaked figure suddenly appears at the edge of the distant trees and the lumbering figure starts splashing, wading through the wet field carrying a huge sack. The figure is totally unaware he's being watched and tracked by a huge dog that is larger than a male black panther.

The rest of this story unfolds in split seconds. Allie in her time with us hardly barks more than a one bark notice and has never shown any aggressive behavior. I could hardly believe what happened next. I realize this dark figure is a duck poacher who is setting decoys for an early morning hunt poaching on our property. As I yell, "get off our property", I realize that Allie is barking furiously, growling, and to my horror is airborne soaring over the canal. I anticipate pulling her out of the canal but my fears are allayed as I see her running, hardly touching the water and closing now within seconds to the dark retreating figure, who realizes he is being chased and frantically is trying to reach the barbwire fence that he cut. Allie has covered what would be a deep-water covered football field in seconds. She is within several yards from the poacher when I realize I cannot let her take this figure down for several reasons— mostly her safety. She is going to defend me at all cost; I can hear it in her continued angry barking as she pursues this fiend. This frantically stumbling cumbersomely dressed poacher knows this isn't a miniature birddog chasing him and probably can't image what animal can run across 8-10 inches of water that fast.

At the top of my lungs I yell the cue, "Allie-Allie"! In midair Allie turns and starts running back to me. Relieved that Allie is coming back,

I begin to worry whether Allie can find me, because the moon reflection is reversed. I continue cheering her on with my voice, but I wonder if she can again clear the canal. There is a bridge a short distance away, but Allie is almost back to me and I don't want her confused. I stay put and keep calling to her when out of the darkness she flies back across the canal and is sitting next to me looking expectantly with her cute soft puppy-like eyes as if to say, "Well, where's my treat?" I exhale and reach in my pocket and hand her a treat. Everything is as it was —a beautiful quiet evening, with a splendid moon shining over the wetland.

We stand there, Allie relishing her treat and I am totally shaken and incredulous about what transpired. Since I started teaching behavior modification to people and animals, I am always amazed about how strong cues become even in a tense situation. Besides the strength of reinforced behavior, there are some very important secondary or resulting cues that often aren't obvious. They are the less systematically taught skills that are created in an encouraging learning environment. Over a period of time a positive connection becomes equally as strong as the taught cues; they are called the relationship, which is created along with the positive times of being together. Without doubt the rewards connected with cues are strong as exemplified with Allie and important, but the small less obvious experiences are even stronger.

Obviously the positive cue training was very important in this happening, but there were also the hours I spend with Allie in positive unstructured times that are perhaps inexplicably as important to the cues I taught her that explain what transpired; this is true for **Positive Horses.**

Key Points

- Teaching cues are important for the safety of our beloved animals.
- Teaching cues not only are important to keep them safe but to create a positive bond.
- The positive teaching environment becauses a powerful influence to making teaching cues more effective but also creating a encouraging relationship.
- Animals and people are aware of the aspects of the teaching environment that are not often obvious.
- Because the cues are taught with a positive method the total horse/rider relationship is also positive.

Books by Patti Dammier PhD

Xerxio, Lusitano from Portugal, taken in Barcelona, Spain

Dr. Patti Dammier has three books devoted to describing the science of training horses based on the method of using behavior modification, which outlines the specific sequences that allows behavior change. According to Kazdin (1994) "behaviors operate based on the environment and have consequences that affect the likelihood that they are performed in the future" (p. 25). Understanding those behavioral sequences produces the likelihood of producing calm positive horse performance–**Positive Horses.**

All of her books stress "A positive method for training horses". It's not enough to read oversimplified catchy techniques, some that have little to do with the total goal of training horses, which not only includes working with horses on the ground but also being ridden. She explains how the common rider aids, which if not understood often lead to the use of excessive force. Even though positive reinforcers (which include effective food rewards) rider aids are rarely discussed, because they demand a more difficult explanation. Rider aids are merely neutral tools until used by the rider. Dr. Dammier describes all the methods used by riders and explain them so they are understood in a positive context.

Behavior Modification for Horses: A positive Method for Training Horses
There are two published editions: 2001 and 2019

Horse Makeovers: A Positive Method for Training Horses: 2014

Positive Horses: A positive Method Using Behavior Modification: 2019

All three books describe the method of using behavior modification for specifically training horses and case studies with explanations of the positive use of rider aids.

Afterword

This book *Positive Horses* continues the methodology described in my first two books: *Behavior Modification for Horses* and *Horse Makeovers*. The books including this edition are separated into sections that explain the techniques of training using behavior modification. The other sections describe case studies that use these methods and give examples of how to use these techniques in a variety of equestrian and riding situations.

Much of the equestrian literature describes what are advertised as natural and positive methods, but they lack any systematic approach and the techniques use unspecified emotional descriptions. There is over a hundred years of scientific research that supports how animals learn, so to ignore this in favor of unsubstantiated marketed hype is unfortunate.

Behavior modification has been criticized as manipulation. The truth is we are all influenced by the environment and to let it occur randomly or by chance risks an unfortunate outcome. The positive effect that is a an outcome of using the positive method of behavior modification is that besides learning effective cues that make the training environment enjoyable and safe, the individual in their learning environment has a positive outlook to all associated to this learning setting.

Here are several examples:

a. When working with young children to increase their motivation to learn to read, reading coaches were taught to merely repeat the correct answer, have the child say the correct answer, and respond with various positive statements connected with real performance. The children who had been unhappy with reading lessons looked forward to their reading sessions. This is an example of secondary reinforcers that create the less the tangible positive learning environment, but an extremely important outcome.

b. The horses on the farm trained by me respond to my presence even when I'm not giving cues. It's become an interesting aside to the training that because this factor is so strong that even the sound of my voice gets their attention. They recognize my voice so if I make a certain sound they listen. This is partially due to the fact I trained my horses unlike the horses I work with and their owners. My horses have come to connect me with a positive occurrence together thus creating **positive horses.**

c. This positive aspect of creating a positive learning setting became obvious with the story of Allie. The part of her responding to the taught cues learned with primary or food reinforcers was not so surprising. The part that even surprised me was the positive attitude of Allie during a highly stressful occurrence.

Key Points

- Beside the positive method of behavior modification there are important aspects to creating positive learning environment.
- The positive learning environment is created by focusing on the rewarding reinforcers, carefully using negative reinforcers-riders aids using them sparingly and releasing them as soon as the horse responds
- Careful use of aversive control called punishment—better use of rewarding incompatible behavior. Remember kids can't be running around yelling and be sitting down quietly reading a book. Horses can't be nipping, moving around and standing at the cue to stand at the same time. Allie can't be jumping at me and sitting by my side. So rather than smacking Allie when she would get excited and jump—all 180-solid- pounds of muscle— I taught her same hand cue as the horses; in this case the cue meant sit.

About the Author

Dr. Patricia "Patti" Dammier relies on over thirty-five years of experience in horse training, professional research, and education to offer an innovative approach that uses scientific evidence to teach basic principles of basic behavior change. Besides her experience training horses, her degrees include a PhD in psychology and a Master's degree in Education, specializing in curriculum development and teaching behavior modification programs to create optimal learning environments.

Concerned about the lack of behavioral literature describing the training of horses, Patti is presently concentrating on collecting data and writing about the use of behavioral science for training horses. Behavior modification brings the dependability of a consistent approach to develop a positive approach to learning and training environments. Horses need to have the comfort of knowing what is expected and the consistency of methodical training instead of the latest fad. Living more than half of her life in Europe afforded Patti the opportunity to study riding in the best schools in Spain, Portugal, England, and Germany. Not only does she have riding and training expertise but the knowledge to use behavior modification to implement those skills and create curriculum.

Quality education consists of knowledge and not a series of faddish shortcuts. Knowledge of the basic principles of behavior modification provides the groundwork to teach horses the behavior we want and make our relationships with horses more positive.

If you would like to know more about behavior modification for horses check the internet site at: http://www.gotcarrots.com

Got Carrots? ® is a national trademark.

Glossary

Aversive control or punishment An unpleasant consequence following a behavior that results in termination of the behavior.

Behavior A single event of observable or measurable behavior.

Behavior Modification The application of the principles of conditioning to changing behavior.

Behavior science The systematic study of the behavior of organisms.

Horses like all animals, including us, tend to repeat pleasurable happenings and avoid those that are unpleasant.

Behaviorism An approach to psychology that studies observable behavior and the role of the environment as a determinant of behavior.

Behavior modification A system for the appraisal and change of behavior.

Consequence Outcomes or results of actions and behavior.

Contingencies The conditions under which specific reinforcer are applied to behavior.

Classical conditioning The systematic and sometimes by chance application of contingencies to behavior that are reflexes. For horses it is important that the flight reflex isn't paired with a chance cue.

Cue An event that signals that a particular behavior will be reinforced.

It's useful to create cues that may be used both on the ground and in the saddle.

Environment The surroundings that support learning. When beginning a task the environment is created so that the desired behavior is promoted.

Ethology The study of animals to determine genetic or environmental causes for behaviors.

Goals A broadly described statement or aim about a behavioral activity. Often these goals are so broadly stated that it would be difficult to make them obtainable. An example for a beginning rider would be: "I will ride my horse in a local schooling show".

Half-Halt A series of rider aids that intermittently signals the horse to move forward and stop forward movement. The horse learns this subtle set of signals because the rider immediately releases the uncomfortable pressure upon yielding. For some disciplines the reins take contact and totally release the contact upon performance.

For the dressage horse, this set of signals is complicated, because the horse has to learn to stay in light contact after the signal with the totally —hopefully quiet rider.

The half-halt for the dressage rider is a sophisticated cue that takes patient training, which can't resort to force.

Incompatible Behavior Two completely different behaviors can't coexist. If the desired behavior is reinforced until it increases, the opposite undesirable incompatible behavior decreases.

Natural reflexes or instincts Responses such as salivation, breathing, suckling, and flight. They are considered behaviors necessary for survival.

Negative reinforcers An aversive event that when stopped increases the response that terminate the aversive event. Rider aids are negative reinforcers that when immediately released, increased the behavior that stops the mildly unpleasant effect (when correctly performed).

Objectives The observable behavior single event or action that leads to the goal. A useful objective state includes a description of what the learner is expected to do, conditions and the level of competence (Mager, p.52).

Operant conditioning The systematic arranging or operations that produce a behavior that is created through the application contingencies that allow new behavio4 to be formed.

Primary reinforcers For horses, primary reinforcers are food because it doesn't depend on learning for its reinforcing attributes.

Reinforcers Those consequences that strengthen the response or increase the rate of responding.

Rewards of positive reinforcers A pleasurable consequence after a behavior that will increase the rate of responding.

Stimulus A signal or some kind of cue present—could be visual, sound, or smell.

Schedules of reinforcement A decision made about how many or which response will be reinforced.

Secondary reinforcers. In contrast to primary reinforcers, secondary reinforcers depend on learning. They are cues or symbols that have been attached to primary reinforcers by training and previous experience. The pat-pat/good horse becomes a secondary reinforcer when the pat-pat was previous done while giving a primary reinforcer, example-a carrot.

Successive approximation Responses that are reinforced as they more closely approached the final desired behavior.

References

American Hungarian Horse Association. (n.d.). Retrieved June 2, 2019, from https://www.hungarianhorseassociation.com/history

Barrey. C. (n.d.). *Scientists and horseman speak out against unlicensed trainers.* Retrieved July 10, 2019 from http://www.lrgaf.org/training/academics.htm

Beck, A. (n.d.). *White Horse Farm Equine Ethology Project in Northland/ New Zealand,* Retrieved July 10, 2019, from https://www.equinesciencesacademy.com/main/student/

Bolt, H. (1978). *Das Dressur Pferd (The Dressage Horse)* Germany: Edition Haberbeck.

Dammier, P. (2001). *Behavior modification for horses.* IN: Iuniverse.

Dammier, P. (2014). *Horse makeovers.* IN: Iuniverse.

Dammier, P. (2019). *Behavior modification for horses.* IN: Iuniverse.

De la Guérinière, F. R._(1994*). School of horsemanship._ London: J. A. Allen & Co.

De la Guérinière, F. R._(1733). *Ecole de cavalerie._ Paris: Collombat.

Edwards, E. H. (1991). *The Ultimate horse book.* NY: Dorling Kndersley.

Gianoli, L. (1969). *Horses and horsemanship through the ages.* New York: Crown Publishers, Inc.

Heinrich, R. (2001). *Schooling horses in hand.* VT: Trafalgar Square Publishing.

Kazdin, A. E. (1975). *Behavior modification in applied settings.* Homewood, II: The Dorsey Press.

Klimke, R. (1969). *Cavaletti.* Canaan, NY: J.A. Allen & Co.

Kurrel (2018). Lluet Horse and Pony Trust Retrieved June 2018 from www.lluesthorseandponytrust.co

Mager, R. F. (1997). *Preparing instructional objectives.* Atlanta, GA: The Center for Effective Performance, Inc.

Mueller, P. Chrzanowska, A., & Piscula,W. (2016). A Critical Comment on the Monty Roberts Interpretation of Equine Behavior. *Pyshcology,7,* 480-487. http://dx.doi.otg/10,4236/psych.2016.74049

Podhajsky, A (1976). *The art of dressage.* Garden City, NY: Doubleday & Company.

Podhajsky, A (1974). *The riding teacher.* London: Harrap & Co.

Podhajsky, A (1969). *My horses, my teachers.* Garden City, NY: Doubleday & Company, Inc.

Podhajsky, A. (1965). *The complete training of horse and rider.* Garden City, NY: Doubleday & Company, Inc.

Olivera, N. (1976). *Reflections on equestrian art.* London: J. A. Allen.

Skinner, B.F. (1953). *Science and human behavior.* New York: The Free Press.

Skinner, B.F. (1974). *About behaviorism.* New York: Alfred A. Knopf.

Stanier, S. (2001). *The art of long reining.* London: J.A. Allen.

Vavra, R. (1977). *Equus-the creation of a horse.* New York: William Morrow & Company, Inc.

Weiten, W. (1989). *Psychology themes and variations.* Pacific Grove, CA: Brooks/Cole Publishing Company.

Xenophon. *On horsemanship.* Written in fourth century B.C.

Index

A

Antecedent 5
aversive xxiii, 7, 8, 23, 112, 117
Aversive 6, 7, 115

B

Behavior, 5
behavior analysis xviii, xxi, xxiii, 69
behavior modification xix, xxi, xxii, 4, 6, 8, 30, 91, 106, 109, 110, 111, 112, 113

C

CarriageTraining xx, 51
Classical conditioning 116
consequence 5, 6, 7, 22, 24, 115, 117
Consequence 5, 11, 13, 19, 33, 36, 37, 115
correct behavior. *See* behavior
critical thinking xxiii, 44
Critical thinking xxiii
crupper 52, 53, 65, 78
Cue 5, 11, 13, 19, 36, 37, 47, 92, 95, 98, 103, 116

D

Dammier, P 119

E

environment xix, xxiii, 8, 15, 16, 20, 42, 76, 91, 92, 95, 97, 98, 103, 106, 107, 109, 111, 112, 115, 116
ethology 41

F

fad xix, 113
Four cues 101

G

goal xix, xx, xxi, 61, 73, 110, 117
goals xvii, xix, 116

H

half-halt 6, 27, 34, 35, 37, 59, 116
hereditary 50
Horse Makeover xx
horse training xviii, xix, xx, xxii, 2, 3, 14, 20, 27, 30, 34, 35, 37, 39, 41, 42, 53, 85, 91, 113
Horse training xvii, xxii
horse whispering 42
hype xviii, xxii, 40, 41, 111

dressage 28, 31, 36, 40, 44, 49, 50, 66, 67, 94, 100, 116
Driving a Cart 47

I

incompatible behavior 11, 88, 90, 112, 117
Incompatible behavior 8, 88
Incompatible Behavior 117

L

learning xviii
learning theory xxi, 1, 44
longe 14, 20, 25, 26, 27, 28, 35, 51, 52, 53, 54, 55, 57, 59, 60, 61, 62, 63, 65, 66, 70, 71, 72, 73, 74, 75, 76, 77, 80, 81, 98, 99, 100, 101
long rein lesson 78

M

marketing copy 41
mystery methods xvii
mysticism xviii

N

natural 43, 49, 50, 95, 111
negative xxiv, 5, 6, 7, 9, 19, 20, 22, 24, 32, 34, 35, 36, 37, 85, 87, 88, 90, 112, 117
Negative 5, 7, 19, 33, 36, 37, 47, 117
Negative Reinforcer 19, 33, 36
Negative reinforcers 5, 33, 37, 117

O

objective xix, xx, 26, 63, 117
operant conditioning xxi, 3

P

Podhajsky 31, 35, 120
Positive consequences 1

Positive Horse xvii
positive methods. xviii, xxiv, 93
Positive Reinforcement 2, 3
Positive reinforcers 4
Primary reinforcers 37, 92, 95, 96, 117
Punishment 6, 7

R

research. *See* behavior modification
Reward 4, 5, 7, 13, 92, 95
rewards xvii, xix, xxi, 1, 2, 3, 4, 6, 10, 15, 16, 19, 22, 23, 24, 29, 30, 32, 36, 37, 42, 56, 69, 72, 73, 92, 96, 106, 110
Rider aids 5, 37, 110, 117
risk management xix, xxii, 62, 86
Risk Management xxi, 84

S

safety xvii, xxiii, 3, 7, 11, 56, 59, 62, 65, 67, 69, 70, 72, 74, 75, 97, 103, 104, 105, 107
secondary reinforcers 37, 96, 97, 112, 118
Secondary reinforcers 92, 96, 118
sound. *See* cues
species specific behavior 3, 40
specific behaviors xix
stand-in reward 4, 5, 10
Successive approximation 118

V

visual 97. *See* cues

X

Xenophon 121

Printed in the United States
By Bookmasters